The Autonomous Image

The Autonomous Image

CINEMATIC NARRATION AND HUMANISM

A. J. Prats

THE UNIVERSITY PRESS OF KENTUCKY

Copyright © 1981 by The University Press of Kentucky

Scholarly publisher for the Commonwealth,
serving Bellarmine University, Berea College, Centre
College of Kentucky, Eastern Kentucky University,
The Filson Historical Society, Georgetown College,
Kentucky Historical Society, Kentucky State University,
Morehead State University, Murray State University,
Northern Kentucky University, Transylvania University,
University of Kentucky, University of Louisville,
and Western Kentucky University.

Editorial and Sales Offices: The University Press of Kentucky
663 South Limestone Street, Lexington, Kentucky 40508-4008
www.kentuckypress.com

Cataloging-in-Publication Data is available from the Library of Congress.

ISBN 978-0-8131-1406-4 (cloth: alk. paper)

This book is printed on acid-free paper meeting
the requirements of the American National Standard
for Permanence in Paper for Printed Library Materials.

∞

Manufactured in the United States of America.

Member of the Association of
American University Presses

CONTENTS

To WALTER C. FOREMAN, JR.
as the meager return for his
all too generous silent partnership

PREFACE

Early in his *Adventures of Ideas,* Alfred North Whitehead writes, "In every age of well-marked transition there is the pattern of habitual dumb practice and emotion which is passing, and there is oncoming of a new complex of habit. Between the two lies a zone of anarchy, either a passing danger or a prolonged welter involving misery of decay and zest of young life. In our estimate of these agencies everything depends upon our standpoint of criticism. In other words, our history of ideas is derivative from our ideas of history, that is to say, upon our own intellectual standpoint." The general critical standpoint in this essay assumes without apologies that the movies are among but a handful of momentous events—worthy of rank with relativity, quantum theory, and what A. O. Lovejoy called "the great revolt against dualism"—that make of the twentieth century an age of transition. In the widest possible sense, this study is an assessment of the movies as contributors to one of the most creative revolutions in Western history.

In a more specific way, the fundamental value of the movies as events capable of reshaping contemporary man's vision of himself and his world resides in *the liberation of the image* from the almost twenty-five hundred years of thralldom to which it had been subjected since Plato's time. The autonomous visual event is today one of the great ways of entering into the adventures of ideas. The concerns of this essay revolve around the possibility, the very strong possibility, that the movies may bear the seeds for the fulfillment—indeed, for the extension and expansion—of the most cherished human values of the Western tradition.

With this possibility in mind, I have aimed at illustrating and clarifying, through the examination of specific movies, the phenomenon of cinematic narration as it grows to form a coherent complex of creative habit. Accordingly *narrative* and *narration* are the central terms of this study. For narrative and narration are the broadest possible terms for the characterization of actions, feelings, and thoughts. No action, no manifestation of feelings, no expression of thought, can exist without a story, that is, without the lively enactment of a relation.

As man moves and grows into a new millenium, he does so as an image of his own and the world's making. The movies are an indispensable part of that movement, of that growth. They have revolutionized art as well as thought about art; they have revolutionized life. None but the blindest will ignore the bare phenomenon of the movies. And the critic, a bit wiser perhaps, will come to be aware that he cannot ignore the humanism begotten of cinematic narration.

Every age of transition requires that the almost anarchic zest of young life be somehow rescued from the passing moment in which it exhibits the sheer exuberance of its novelty. To the critic falls the task of systematic inquiry into the values of that novelty of expression. Yet there is in this essay no guiding theory properly so called, that is, no prescription as to what movies are, ontologically, and no concept dogmatically insisting on what they ought to be, for prescriptive theory serves to mark the end of a transitional age, while dogmatism kills the age's adventurous drive by inhibiting its potentialities for growth. I wish to avoid any such fatal results.

Broadly speaking, the period of well-marked transition immediately following World War II saw the movies turn into events of a "self-conscious" expression of zest of young life through the agency of the color image. The growing preponderance of color movies in the postwar era marks more than a technological advance, more than a box-office necessity. It marks a further development in the process of the image's liberation. It is no coincidence that all the movies discussed in this essay have some part of their action narrated in black-and-white. One of the major interests of this study is to see how, in each movie, black-and-white images function in relation to color ones.

In black-and-white, the movies could still be thought of as coincidental disclosures of the dualism of classical and Cartesian thought. They could accordingly remain shackled to the archaic modes of thought that had for centuries made the image the mirror held up to nature, and that had made "Spectacle" the gratuitous feature of narrative. Self-divided, the black-and-white image mirrored the moral and esthetic dualism of the prewar world itself.

The transition to color announced that here at long last was the image in all its dynamically unified variety; that here was the moral and esthetic model by which the divisiveness and decay of contemporary political doctrines and philosophical camps might be overcome. Here was democratic pluralism turned esthetic event. Here was Bergson's dream of the "spiritualization of matter" made an actuality. It is much too early for a prescriptive, all-encompassing theory of the movies. The living image, begotten of a new imagination, will not, indeed cannot, *stand* reduction for the sake of theoretical safety. The systematic celebration of the values that the movies have just begun to unfold will have to do. In every age of transition the effort at systematization is the alternative to both hermetic dogmatism and sheer anarchic zest.

Within such a historical context, it is clear that the criticism the movies require is a descriptive (as opposed to a demonstrative) form of thought directed by the various and specific narrative methods that a few discrete cinematic events can readily reveal. Most other forms of criticism involve a retreat into the dim light of abstractions and generalities, a retreat from the enlightening cinematic facts.

Yet all critical inquiries with more than a passing concern for the humanism inherent in their subject matter bear an implicit ideal, bear a broader vision of that effort of thought which is in the end the critic's most valuable gift to his reader. The student of the movies who is well acquainted with "film theories" and their applications will find little that is familiar in the method of criticism in this study, will find nothing that directly confirms the "theory" he most favors. He will no doubt find that the major premises and assumptions of a great number of them are implicitly examined, but will undoubtedly be frustrated when he finds that there is not a single textual indebtedness to the theorist of his predilection. And perhaps he will be more frustrated still to find that there is here—by chance more than by choice—an implicit rejection of those major premises and assumptions which form the base, the sometimes too rigid base, of most "film theories."

The guiding ideal of this study is an earnest hope that the serious,

open-minded student of the movies—the student with a keen sense
of their importance in contemporary life—may come to see in this
essay an open-ended dialog. The ideal, in short, takes the form of an
appeal to the student's own sense of adventure into new modes of
perception and thought about and from the movies.

Ideas inhere in facts. When the ideas are faithful to the facts that
engendered them, "all" that is left is the new fact, that is to say, the
original fact in all its experiential integrity now made richer, now
made more appealing to our zest for adventure in the realm of
human values. It is the function, nay, the duty of any critical inquiry
to enrich the object of its study. The most bountiful harvest of
thought in ages of well-marked transition is not the result of asking
of the object of inquiry, What is it? but, What does it do? and How
does it do what it does? And even afterward, important questions
remain to be asked, such as, What is to be done with the esthetic
deed? What new human values does it express? How has the event
come to narrate a novel relation between itself and life? As a sort of
warning, the less adventurous reader ought to be told forthwith that
he may find the present inquiry a bit too "metaphysical." But let his
fear and distrust of metaphysics be dispelled: "Metaphysics,"
William James wrote, "means nothing but an unusually obstinate
effort to think clearly."

In the process of thinking clearly about the four movies with
which it deals, this study becomes a narrative all its own; it becomes
a story, which, like the movies themselves is not bound to be "true."
Instead, it sees, it fleshes out, and it lauds the new possibilities for
values in the cinematic events. Moreover this study does not posit
an *ex post facto* conclusion where all that has been said in the text is
compacted into a definitive summarizing statement. If anything, the
Epilog raises more questions than it can hope to answer.

Scant indeed is the list of presupposed items in this investigation.
The first of these is that the essential feature of the image's liberation is to be seen in the fact that the cinematic image *moves*. (Hence
the preference herein for the term "movie," as opposed to "film.")
The second is that movies are primarily visual events. This presupposition implies no so-called purism. Purism died with the advent of
the talkies, and out of that death a new narrative possibility was
born, namely, the new function of verbal narration as it coexists with
and is modified by the moving image. The third is color, which,

being a further development in the integrity of the liberated image, is generally speaking a postwar phenomenon. The fourth assumption is this, that the cinematic and humanistic values of the moving image in color are discovered in the details of movie sequences and in the adequately described relations of those details to one another. The fifth is the inadequacy of language for the proper expression of the immediate cinematic fact. The sixth presupposition, however, is that descriptive language can to a great extent compensate for the loss of the immediacy of the moving image. Seventh, and last, is the assumption that each of the four movies discussed in this essay is both "intensive" and "extensive"—that is, each movie is capable of being both itself and the welter of possibilities for cinematic and humanistic values that each can yield. Hence the emphasis on *growth* in this essay, which is in direct contrast to emphasis on similarities.

Generally speaking, the method of investigation for each of the movies has its origin in a specific *model* of narration found in a sequence or a contrast of sequences in the movie itself. To focus on a model of narration is critically to follow the image's lead; it is to go as directly as possible at the whole action through the unfolding relations and narrative functions of one of the organic components of the action.

The first chapter is in effect the introduction, for the examination of *Fellini: A Director's Notebook* introduces the narrative values that are explored further in the subsequent chapters. It introduces the contrasts, interactions, and reciprocal modifications of these narrative values as well as the intensive and extensive humanism inherent in the cinematic achievement of *Director's Notebook* itself. Also, chapter 1 is an explicit introduction to the historical and intellectual context of the whole book.

An explanation of why the four movies discussed in this study are all made by Italians is almost superfluous. From the fourteenth to the seventeenth century, Italy's history is the narrative of scores of persons whose visual genius, whose zest for adventure, and whose fascination with motion are in effect the roots of the present-day genius of the Italian cinema. But certainly these movies have not been chosen solely because they are Italian-made. And even less is there in this essay an explicit concern with Italian culture and society as it may exhibit itself in the four movies.

Finally, a question may be anticipated with regard to the arrangement of the chapters. If the essay's central theme is the *growth* of cinematic values and the humanism they engender, why doesn't the discussion move from *Blowup* (1966) to *The Clowns* (1970) to *Seven Beauties* (1975) as chronology would seem to require? The first answer—by far the most important—is that genuine novelty does not obey chronology. But it might also be pointed out that the chapter arrangement reflects the historical settings of the movies: *Seven Beauties* begins before World War II, goes through the protagonist's participation in the war, and has its final sequence set in postwar Italy. *Blowup* is a story set in the mid-sixties, *The Clowns* in the early seventies. Perhaps there is more narrative necessity attached to a historical setting than seems at first glance possible.

All public expressions of gratitude suffer from gross omissions. As a person grows, the lines between personal, intellectual, and professional debts cease to have any significance—even if the indebtedness accumulates. This fact gives unity and value to a life, but it also makes the naming of all the particular names as dull and meaningless as one of those unending acceptance speeches at an Academy Awards banquet. I do not forget my gratitude to my friends and colleagues, old and new. And I can only hope that they will settle for a less formal expression of thanks. But the more intimate debts must be acknowledged explicitly. Thus, to Tonya F. Prats, I give much more thanks than those perfunctory ones usually bestowed on a wife. To her I owe the better part of a rather good story. My love to Becky and Agatha for, among other things, growing joyously before my eyes long before I could really see that it was all about change and growth. W. R. Robinson's zest of young life and generosity of mind is an enduring source of inspiration. The unflinching devotion of Olga Prats and Clara Avendaño are, as they always have been, inexhaustible moral resources. And so, in their own ways are the lives of Mariano Prats (1919–1959) and Armando Rodriguez-Cáceres (1893–1963): "Our souls / Are love and a continual farewell." Another immediate and nondischargeable debt is to be found in the dedication of this book.

Chapter 4 of this book appeared in somewhat different form as "An Art of Joy, an Art of Life: The Plasticity and Narrative Methods of *The Clowns*" in *The 1977 Film Studies Annual: Part One, Explorations in National Cinemas*, pp. 143-60; I am grateful to the Redgrave Publishing Company for granting me permission to include it here.

I wish to thank the University of Kentucky Graduate School for a summer research fellowship that allowed me free time for study and writing, and the University of Kentucky Research Foundation for a grant that allowed me to review the movies and make my descriptions more accurate. A special thanks to Katherine Madden of Films, Inc.; to Debbie Bierley, the best typist; and to Frank Leach, who tried his best.

1

The New Narration of Values

FELLINI: A DIRECTOR'S NOTEBOOK

Then, at dawn, as I droned on to myself about
the new form my home town had taken on,
all this unknown Rimini . . . seemed to be trying
to tell me . . . that it had changed and so I had
better change as well.

FEDERICO FELLINI

More than a fresh personal vision of the potentialities of cinematic narration on the part of Federico Fellini himself, *Fellini: A Director's Notebook* is a work that opens up new possibilities for revolutionary narrative directions in the life of the movies.[1] *Director's Notebook* is not, strictly speaking, a documentary; it is not even a documentary of the making of a movie.[2] Nor is it only a movie about a movie—a mere example, that is, of what in movie criticism is currently being called "formal reflexivity."[3] It is more accurate to say that *Director's Notebook* is the story of discovering new narrative possibilities; it is thus the re-formed narrative, initiating the fulfillment of contemporary life's esthetic and moral possibilities. *Director's Notebook* addresses itself directly to man's condition as a narrative creature. It raises the problem of narration as the central humanistic problem facing contemporary man. It "solves" that problem; but it does not do so with the aid of a ready-made narrative premise. On the contrary, it solves the problem through active inquiry into the diversity of relations in which man finds himself to his world.

Director's Notebook begins its journey toward the actualization of new narrative potentialities in a most inauspicious fashion. It begins by taking a trip back, a memory trip, in which Fellini returns to the Mastorna set.[4] Thus as a way of getting on with the story of the new image of man, it "begins" by adopting conventional narrative devices.

In the impersonal style of the guiding narrator in a neoclassical novel, Fellini, a disembodied voice, introduces the "strange, lonely shapes" of the now-abandoned set for a "project"—"The Voyage of G. Mastorna"—which he never completed.[5] It is history that Fellini deals in, not only because he begins his part in the story by letting words do the narrative work, but also because he returns to the past only to contemplate it, not to create from it.

Yet the very first images of Mastorna belie Fellini's intentions merely to review the Mastorna project or to indulge in a sentimental outpouring on the topic of the death of his imaginative capacities. The tall grass has grown around the decaying buildings and the airplane of the set. In the center of the set's "piazza" a horse grazes undisturbed. Accordingly, Fellini's voice, which draws attention to itself as a vehicle for conventional narration, is instantly denied preeminence by the actuality of the image of the natural and the organic that grows to envelop the contrived and the decaying. When juxtaposed to the visual action, the disembodied voice, which appears to be a narrative atavism, in fact makes apparent the intrinsic relation between old and new narrative modes which is the essence of the narrative growth in *Director's Notebook*. The growth—the growth of the grass around the world of artifice, the growth of *Director's Notebook* from "The Voyage of G. Mastorna"—is the actuality.[6] The unique contrasts and juxtapositions of the first episode in themselves contain the intermingling of *cinematic* and *archaic* narration from which the totally new narrative vision of *Director's Notebook* can be seen to emerge.[7]

Because of its episodic structure (see Appendix for a summary), *Director's Notebook* does not reveal a clear-cut line of demarcation between one narrative commitment and another. There is no precise point at which the archaic narration altogether surrenders its narrative energies to cinematic narration. It is accordingly crucial to bear in mind throughout that the distinct narrative modes beget a unified and vital relation to each other, that they engender the creative possibilities and the process of unification whose potential is inherent in the very contrast of the modes themselves. It is also essential to note from the start that narrative unity in *Director's Notebook* is not achieved by the mere arbitrary ascription (by, say, Federico Fellini), of narrational priorities to one set of narrative components over the other. Rather, the interaction involves intrinsic and reciprocal modifications and adaptations of both the conventional and the cinematic modes of narration. This means that the archaic narrative mode reaches the end of its creative capacities or energies only as the *exclusive* mode of narration.

In *Director's Notebook*, then, the image of man in the heat of narrative action is an image *in the making*. Precisely because the contrasting narrative modes of *Director's Notebook* show that in many respects the new grows out of the old and not *ex nihilo*, it is crucial also to attend to the operations of the conventional narration in its changing relations to the cinematic one. Some episodes in *Director's Notebook* are thoroughly based on the old narrative assumptions; on the other hand, some clearly show that their origins lie in the completely new. And still others, of which the opening episode is the clearest example, exhibit both old and new narrative methods simultaneously. Because *Director's Notebook* is the story of the new, born of narrative contrasts (indeed of opposites), the first episode is the model of narration on which the present chapter focuses.

First let us consider the life of the young occupants of the Mastorna set. Their elaborate dress, their heavily made-up faces, their lethargic, aimless movements, and their overcivilized manners readily contrast with the wilderness surrounding the set. Their lives clearly parallel Fellini's own description of the set as having "remained like this, useless and empty"—especially when one of the young hippies says to Fellini that they couldn't leave Mastorna even if they wanted to, because their car has no wheels. Like the mockup of the airplane in which G. Mastorna would have arrived but which now stands supported by wooden beams, the hippies' car is itself a "prop," itself "useless and empty."

As important as the image of man embodied in the hippies is the fact that Fellini's creative predispositions at this time (if indeed he has any), are far from matching the growth and the abundance of natural life surrounding the set. Instead, because Fellini has re-

turned to the Mastorna set, because he has in effect subsumed
imagination under memory, whatever creative inclinations he may
possess turn out to reveal an affinity with the lives of the bohemians.
For the image of man in Mastorna is at odds with the world. It is an
image of man in a place where, as the hippie poet puts it, "nobody
wants to live and nobody likes to work or hates to die." And the poet
continues his lament: "Mastorna, a city that is sad and beautiful, of
that beauty I love above all others, since all it stands for is folly."
The poet then lies down on a bench, saying, "I want to die here in
Mastorna." In Mastorna, man *stands*, that is, he remains motionless, *against* both life and death, each as a negative abstraction.
There is little else for the poet to do but to lie down and pronounce
his own elegy. This is the first time in the action that the archaic
narrative powers (along with their embodiments) turn against
themselves, annihilate themselves.

As for Fellini, his return to Mastorna's "crazy ruins" is for now
merely an implicit acknowledgment of his failure to venture into
new narrative terrain. In fact, Fellini has yet to become an image.
He continues to be a disembodied voice, interrogating the hippies,
holding fast to the traditional separation between the seeing and the
seen, and using the word as mediator between them.

And yet, Fellini's and the hippies' failure to live in even the most
passive of worlds is soon enough turned into an announcement of a
creative triumph. As the poet concludes his oration on the dearth of
life in Mastorna, the natural world gives further evidence of its
capacity to grow. For just at this moment the wind howls and buffets
the faces of the surprised hippies, the snow falls heavily, and the
noise of an airplane flying overhead is heard as the camera looks
straight at the sun behind the clouds. Then the camera cuts away to
the moving mock-up of G. Mastorna's plane.

But shortly thereafter it sees the back of G. Mastorna, who is
dressed in black and carries a briefcase in his left hand, a cello case
in his right. For rather than envision a new narrative from the
miraculous outbreak of energies beyond the control of words (not
the least of which is the action of the camera as it looks straight at the
source of light), Fellini obstinately recreates the old story by cutting
away from the action of the world to the actor. Analytically, divi-
sively, Fellini establishes bipolar categories of narration. Reemerg-
ing, Fellini's voice says over the image of G. Mastorna, "This is

Mastorna, the hero of my film, a cellist. His voyage would have begun like this—an unexpected landing in a strange, dreamlike piazza." Fellini tells the story of the "hero"—the story of the contemporary impossibility of being "larger than life." Moreover, since G. Mastorna is faceless, he is identifiable only through abstractions, that is, through Fellini's voice and through his own profession or social function. The story of the hero is conceived by a subjectively controlling will ("my film"). Fellini therefore arbitrarily ascribes supremacy to an image over which Fellini's own words rule. Here, then, appear in *Director's Notebook* two more of the fundamental ways in which narration can be self-limiting, archaic: first, the creative urge relies on a dominant image; and second, it relies on a possessive or controlling will at the expense of the narrative forces of the world itself.

When these two archaic narrative components are seen together with Fellini's initial recourse to words, his nostalgic fascination with the static and the artificial, and his dependence on a hollow past, they begin to form the mosaic of the old narrative which must be somehow restructured if *Director's Notebook* is to propel itself into a new narrative vision.

Fellini expresses still another narrative atavism in the first episode. It is that ancient narrative rule, the rule of genesis, of a beginning in an absolute time dimension preceded only by chaos, by, in this case, "an unexpected landing." Fellini's announcement that Mastorna's "voyage would have begun like this" fails to generate a transition from word to image, from the abstract identity to the concrete, individual image of G. Mastorna. An image does accompany Fellini's introduction; but the image is as motionless as the Mastorna set, as vapid as the hippies, and as impotent to engender new matrices for a narrative revolution as are Fellini's own archaic narrative devices. The image that Fellini *calls* G. Mastorna is, more precisely speaking, the anti-image. G. Mastorna lacks the most rudimentary form of individuality because he lacks a face. Also, his black clothes and his motionlessness (his "landing") single him out only as an abstraction incapable of enacting the enlightening possibilities of a new image of man.

Thus appearing out of verbal fiat, the anti-image of G. Mastorna is a throwback to the Platonic concept of image in the *Timaeus*, that is, the "image of eternity" that exists as a derivative of logical dialectics.[8] Fellini's image of G. Mastorna, like Plato's "image of eternity," is divorced from all actualities, from all events, save, of course, from Fellini's words, which, in seeking to recreate from the conceptually preexistent, operate not unlike the *logos* that Plato sought to understand rationally.

One more ancient narrative ploy is implicit in the first episode of *Director's Notebook*. It is the notion of narration as consisting exclusively of hard-and-fast logical relations between cause and effect. When G. Mastorna's anti-image appears on the screen, it has been verbally "caused." Therefore Fellini's voice is literally the *voice over* the image. The visible event springs from an omniscient intellect that confers a merely derivative reality upon the image by virtue of the causal powers traditionally ascribed to words. The image is therefore only the copy, the "imitation" of the word. Like the Hebraic Yahweh or like Aristotle's "unmoved mover," Fellini, too, is *ipso facto* separated from the creation by virtue of "higher" intellectual and verbal powers. He too has willed the creation of a "master" image of man that transcendentally imposes the will on the world, the word on the less than perfect. Fellini's anti-image magically arrives in the "dreamlike piazza" or in Eden or in "time" or in the realm of efficient cause—but it never reveals an immanent capacity to extend the creation.

Initially, then, the narrative thrust of *Director's Notebook* discloses a vital interaction between the characteristic components of conventional narration and those of the new narration. This interaction between contrasting narrative components, though at times it creates narrative tension or narrative by dualism, results ultimately in a unity attained through the interaction of the two "sets" of narrative methods.

The basic components of conventional narration in the first episode of *Director's Notebook* can be enumerated and briefly explained as follows: (1) *the word*—taken in all the substantiality and otherworldliness that it traditionally bears, taken, that is, as the primordial instrument of narration; (2) *the past*—here considered as the safety from change made possible by an overintellectualizing and overidealizing memory; (3) *the static*—permanence and certainty, especially with regard to an unchanging "eminent" reality; (4) *the artificial*—or the intellectually derived conviction that art and life do not complement, much less modify, each other; (5) *the dominant image*—an image of man that claims supremacy over others by virtue of its extraneously acquired identity, an identity which robs individual images of their immanent narrative energies and thus of whatever spiritual possibilities may reside in such narrative energies; (6) *subjectivism*—the overweening narrative importance ascribed by Western thought to the ego at least since the seventeenth century, such a narrative importance precluding the narrative energies of the world's "objects"; (7) *the will*—a claim to narrative self-sufficiency, to mastery over the world one narrates; it is worth noting here that at the very end of the first episode, when the English-speaking interviewer/narrator asks Fellini, "And so, Mr. Fellini, you never made 'The Voyage of Mastorna'?" Fellini replies, "No, not yet. But I will do it, it is the story that I prefer the most"; (8) *knowledge*—considered as the primal desire that Aristotle ascribed to all men, as well as in the sense of "experience," traditionally a precondition of all narrative acts; and (9) *the intellect*—the mediating power that analyzes, classifies, categorizes, reduces, and interprets discrete relations, yet leaves such analyses, classifications, and so forth without any sense of their humanistic consequences. So much for now, then, for the basic components of the archaic narrative mode as exhibited in the first episode of *Director's Notebook*. The reliance on logical causality and the emphasis on genesis, along with other functions of archaic narrative to be examined in other episodes, are derivatives of these basic nine constituents.

Each component of conventional narration is actively accompanied in the opening episode of *Director's Notebook* by its cinematic counterpart: (1) *the image*—best described as a functional unit of discrete visual energy; a unit of light made unique, it is simultaneously particle, wave, and quantum, and thus, by extension, the union of matter and spirit, body and soul; (2) *the present*—the unmediated, ever-perishing instant which not only contains, but continually transforms, the past and the future; (3) *motion*—not only physical activity or visual change of location, but the basic phenomenon accounting for creative change and growth; (4) *the organic*—in contrast to *the artificial*, functioning in such a way that each discrete temporal event passes into the world's body and reshapes it, so that there is no fundamental distinction between the

"subject-matter" of art and the "subject-matter" of life; (5) *the individual human image*—which, free from social roles, identities, titles, names, and so forth, is able to enact a process of becoming of
which the most immediate aim, as well as the ultimate aim, is
individuality; (6) *narrative reciprocity*—through which in a world of
ever-changing qualitative relations, the "object," which for the purposes of this essay is the life of images, is an active narrative energy
capable of changing, of narrating, the "subject," capable, that is, of
transforming the "I" that controls into the eye that creates even as it
lets itself be created; (7) *the active world*—in which events cannot
be controlled by the will; (8) *wisdom*—in contrast to knowledge as
an end in itself; *know-how* or the capacity to transform inert knowledge into narrative action; and (9) *the imagination*—the power that
immediately discovers *value* in discrete visual events; the imagination is not only, as Wallace Stevens put it, "the power of the mind
over the possibilities of things,"[9] but also the power of the possibilities of things over the mind.

Such is an analytic account of the two sets of narrative components in *Director's Notebook*, based on the actions of the first episode. Stated more synthetically, a close examination of the action of
its first episode shows that *Director's Notebook* on the one hand
narrates through the archaic notion of creativity based on verbal
powers seeking the thoroughly subjective control of a permanent
conceptual reality, and that on the other it narrates through its
inherent vision of the potentially creative powers of the moving,
organic image of man free to imagine beyond the boundaries of its
given narrative condition. (These creative powers of the moving,
organic image of man are only potentially present in the first episode
because Fellini turned from the action of the world to the actor.) In
whatever way these narrative methods and their components are
described, however, it is crucial to keep in mind that there is overlap, not only, as should be obvious, among the components of each
set, but between the sets themselves. This overlap is an expression
of the interrelatedness of the narrative methods in *Director's
Notebook*.

The narrative constituents of *Director's Notebook* are not
mechanical devices. They are values, whether they belong to the
archaic or to the cinematic narration. Value is *power*—power to
create what is new, what is good and beautiful, as well as power to

confirm creatively and to extend narratively the life of those narrative occasions—no matter how seemingly trivial—which are the very marrow of life. Value is action in its ideal form.

But there are no values apart from the world of fact. The world of fact exists for its own sake. Initially, the welter of discrete facts bears a close kinship with chaos. (Surely in no art form can this be more evident than in the movies, where each frame is different from the one before it.) And because cinematic values emerge from the world of fact, they, too, tend to the chaotic. It is accordingly an unfortunate truth that values and facts, appearing in their sublunary subtlety, are often prey to the derision of tidy minds. When this happens, critical evaluation does not follow the pattern of intrinsic valuation supplied by the inherent relation of facts and values. Evaluation follows instead the ready-made order of the critical mind. The systematization of the experience of change is therefore the method in this inquiry into cinematic values. When systematized according to their own function, facts become a steady disclosure of differences appearing against a continually shifting background of recurrent patterns of value. The discovery of value in the world of fact is an event whose ultimate characterization is process. Thus the idea of a complete and perfect pattern of value is an illusion of the worst sort. It is the tyranny of the intellect over the world of change as well as over the life of the mind.

Accordingly, these "sets" of narrative components and their constituents are only abstract, though initially adequate, expressions of the inherence of values in facts. They are rough patterns of valuations. But the particular facts are what give them their narrative and humanistic relevance as well as their claim to importance as bases for extensive critical evaluations.

Still, the values which this essay extols, celebrates, are primarily the values of the second set, for such values have made possible the humanistic alternatives of the present age. As a whole, however, *Director's Notebook*, like any movie of consequence, exists, narrates, for its own sake, that is, as the activity in process of generating its own relation between facts and values. And the narrative process of *Director's Notebook* denies no value as ultimately irrelevant or totally obsolete. For if it willfully suppressed possibilities for value through the agency of one constituent, it would implicitly abandon the method of narrative contrasts and inevitably suppress the possibilities for value through the agency of that constituent's counter-part. The modification, not the unqualified supremacy, of one set of values, is what is at stake in the method of narrative contrasts.

As is clear later in *Director's Notebook* (in the screen-test episode with Marcello Mastroianni), G. Mastorna would be an image, or more accurately a character, upon which Fellini would gladly impose his own passion for creative control. But *Director's Notebook* is not only the story of the attenuation of the traditional cinematic and dramatic relationships between director and actor; in the process through which Fellini discovers the full humanistic import of the cinematic narrative energies, the tradition of the artist's necessary reliance on extraneous authorities also perishes as a narrative presupposition. In *Director's Notebook* Fellini seeks these extraneous authorities as he attempts to undertake the "voyage in time" presumably preparatory for *Fellini-Satyricon*. These authorities are Professor Genius and the professor of archeology.

Genius's appearance onscreen is readily analogous to G. Mastorna's several episodes earlier. It is true that Genius's face is what the camera sees first. But as the appearance of G. Mastorna froze the newly awakened dynamism of the camera at the Mastorna set, so Genius's image is trapped in a freeze-frame long enough for Fellini to introduce him formally: "Genius. His name is Professor Genius. He is a very sensitive clairvoyant, and tonight he will try to make a contact with the invisible presences that swarm about us." Again the disembodied voice introduces the static and the decadent. In the car, Genius's still image moves only after Fellini stops talking. But no sooner does he move than Genius starts talking incessantly, frivolously, now in Italian, now in broken English. As Fellini would like to have had happen with G. Mastorna, his voice-over narration has been successfully assimilated by the character he introduces.

While the car moves, Genius's head is turned toward the back seat, where Fellini, Marina Boratto, and Bernardino Zapponi sit. Appropriately, Genius is looking back—back to the director, the script girl, and the writer, whose questions about the past he must answer. Not surprisingly, it is Fellini who asks the question showing the greatest intellectual bias: "Genius, tell us, how often have you seen these real ancient Romans?" Fellini wants to be *told* about reality. Through Genius's agency Fellini searches for the "material cause" from which he can, presumably in *Fellini-Satyricon*, create his "efficient" forms. Furthermore, reality is unmistakably identified with the past. In other words, for now the function of the action is to "see" a fixed historical reality at the expense of the literally moving present. Relying on a mediating power (Genius as "medium") Fellini subsequently orders the driver to stop the car so that Genius may "see." And so once more, as in Mastorna, Fellini arrives at a place shot through with dead history.

Genius sees nothing creative in the cemetery where they stop. He first *tells* of seeing. For example, he tells of seeing the bones of the lions, but actually he has to grope blindly about the ancient wall, and then just as blindly he has to interpret the "substance" that he touches. Genius "sees" verbally. He is therefore at best the bearer of the traditional way of seeing in terms of "eidetic images." In a word, Genius's vision is *metaphorical*.

His hermeneutics acquire still more arcane properties when his secretary, turning to the camera, repeats Genius's explanations of his visions. Genius says that the bones of the animals are buried "about twenty meters" down. The secretary, addressing the camera: "Twenty meters?" Or again, Genius: "Seems to be old bones, . . . I'd say of lions." The secretary, again looking at the camera: "Lions?" More than just a deferential attitude on the secretary's part, his repetition of Genius's words makes him the mediator for the mediator (Genius), as well as the mediator for the pathetically stupid camera, itself for now the victim of the venture into the unseen. Each mediating act becomes an obstacle to the visual adventure that presumably directs Fellini's inquiry.

And when Genius asks for Marina's assistance because he needs to be "charged by the fluid of a young virgin," still nothing creative happens. Instead Genius releases his hold on Marina and collapses to the ground in a masturbatory fit, presumably a "trance," that, again presumably, transports him into a vision of "the family of Flavia," "without eyes, blinded by the emperor," as Genius's secretary translates for the camera. The camera, however, sees nothing but a marble bust in a mist-covered field. It sees the severed head lacking a body, the image that clearly recalls the wide-open head prop that Marina had discarded in mock-repulsion in that other "graveyard," the Mastorna prop room.

Much more inhibitive than Fellini's nostalgic visit to the prop room, Genius's visit to "the real past," allows him to "see" only what is itself blind and motionless. Now forced to listen to the secretary's translation of Genius's words, the camera is told that Genius "is going farther back in the past, to Republican Rome." This time Genius claims to see three dead brothers; the camera can see only three shrouded, faceless, and motionless shapes standing in a foggy field. The ghostly, motionless images that Genius leads the camera to see are veiled, and the veil itself is a conventional metaphor for imperfect vision.

Such are the only images to be seen when the intellect mediates the immediate. Through the agency of this ironic genius, of this ironic man of "generation and birth," the present is an insignificant noumenal universe whose unchanging eminent reality is at odds with a phenomenal world. Genius "sees" (and forces the camera to "see") the anti-image; for his "real" ancient images are as dead and as faceless as is Fellini's personal vision of G. Mastorna. "Reality" is death.

This is again true when the next authority, the professor of archeology, takes Fellini and the camera into the subterranean darkness; or rather, to be more precise, when Fellini forces the professor to take him into the past, saying, "I think this subway ride can help me find the atmosphere I want for my film." In this episode the narrative is once more propelled, loosely speaking, by the old-world notion that it is essential humanistically to appeal to and thoroughly to know the past before a new event can occur. Implicit in the appeal to the past is the still more inhibitive notion that the past exists unqualified by the present, that it is an a priori concept from which to elicit an archetype to which the present is shackled. Not surprisingly Fellini tells the professor, "To me the subway is like a catacomb." He cannot envision the subway as a source of motion on the one hand, and the catacombs as the receptacle of the dead on the other. Like a good intellectual, comparing at all costs even those things that do not belong in the same class, and thus ignoring differences, Fellini "sees" the present as the mere repetition of the past. Thus it is Fellini's "will" that controls the narrative process in the subway episode.

Earlier in the episode, at the café where Fellini and his crew meet the professor, Fellini introduces the professor to Pasqualino

De Santis, the cameraman. Fellini then says to the professor, "Don't be afraid, he will make you look very handsome." Fittingly, however, on the way down the steps leading to the subway, at the moment that Fellini draws his analogy between the subway and the catacombs, the camera sees only the professor's and Fellini's shadows projected against the wall alongside the staircase. Condemned to Fellini's "will" from the beginning, the camera eye cannot "make" the professor look "handsome." Indeed, the camera eye is not free to see: before recording the shadows of the two dominant images, the camera picks up both Fellini and the professor as they begin their descent into the subway, and suddenly Fellini, half turning around to De Santis, angrily orders him to stop photographing his bald spot.

But the camera may, because Fellini so wills it, listen. Thus when the professor attempts rather unsuccessfully, to tell Fellini of his discovery in 1948 of an ancient civilization, Fellini stops him, saying, "Excuse me, Professor . . . repeat again, looking in the camera." Later, during the subway ride, Fellini once more interrupts the professor's dissertation: "Speak a little louder because the noise of the train is covering all your words. And look in the camera, please." The camera here is the instrument for memory; it is a voice recorder only superfluously registering the image, because the image, Fellini has implied, has no basic, that is, no historical, value. The recording function of the camera (in the root sense of the verb "record," that is, *recordāri*, to remember), is now even more of an obstacle in the way of the cinematic narrative forces than it was in the Genius episode.

Consider how the professor takes the historical voyage to its terminus. Before the subway ride begins, the professor says to Fellini, "Underneath this subway—I want you to remember this, it's very fascinating—there are traces of an earlier world than that of Rome." He adds that the vestiges of this civilization are found in "layers" (two below the subway, two above). Here, as well as during the subway ride, the archaic narrative energies themselves are attenuated, for the ancient civilizations are vicious abstractions from which the camera can create nothing. The civilizations are not named, they are not even linked, as are all civilizations, to foundation narratives such as those in Genesis or the *Timaeus* or the *Aeneid*. And this trip into prehistory, indeed into prenarrative

darkness, this ironic if thoroughly traditional concept of the existence of a primal void, is the event to be recorded, "remembered"
by the camera. By taking a trip into prehistory *Director's Notebook*
hits upon the *principium* of traditional narration, namely, upon the
presumptuously self-sufficient word lacking a reference, a datum, a
consequent, even an accident, but lacking, above all, a relation to a
concrete act in the world. In the beginning are the professor's
words, but they beget nothing.

The camera, however, foils both the professor's and Fellini's perverse intentions to turn it into a tool for the memory of what can
never have happened. Well into the historical tour, the professor
says: "Now we're in the heart of the imper. . . ." Abruptly, the camera abandons the professor in midsentence. The train momentarily
goes into a dark station, and out of the darkness miraculously
emerge the images of men and women in colorful Roman togas and
in the uniforms of Roman legionnaires. Thus where Genius's ironic
vision had at least led the camera to a bare simulacrum of images
(the bust and the three veiled ghosts), the professor's history, ever
leading the camera eye into the heart of narrative darkness, requires
that the camera itself make a narrative quantum leap, as it were, if
only that it may save its own narrative capacities for later development.

At the sudden sight of these human images, the professor's intellectual smugness disappears. Now visibly confused, he asks, as if
speaking to himself, "What's happened?" He is at a loss to account
for the outbreak of concrete, particular images which are not verbal
consequents, but which are instead revealed by the bright light that
shines on the faces of each even as the train passes them by. To add
to the professor's disturbed sense of order, the images are inarticu-
late. They do not explain or justify their existence. In their presentational immediacy they "only" look at the camera, confirming the
genius, the creative spirit, of the individual relation between the
seeing and the seen. For instance, sitting casually on a bench
alongside the subway wall, one woman, who is dressed in a vivid red
toga, looks straight at the camera. Some of the men utter incoherent
sounds or gesture with their hands in a form of prelinguistic communication which clearly denies the narrative primacy of the word.

Also, the visual present asserts itself as a power beyond Fellini's
and the professor's control. Thus "time" ceases to have the dis-

jointed yet absolute referential quality with which the professor's history, as well as Fellini's own insistence on the past as the exclusive source for creation, have sought to endow it. While the camera sees the human images that line the subway wall, it lives up to Einstein's assertion that "every reference-body . . . has its own particular time." In other words, camera eye and images operate homogeneously, unmindful, in effect, of the intellectual inclinations of both Fellini and the professor. The professor's question ("What's happened?") is answered in his own terms, with a "happening," with an *event in time*. "There is time," Whitehead wrote, "because there are happenings, and apart from happenings there is nothing."[10]

The *terminus ad quem* of the archaic narrative as witnessed in the two episodes discussed above is the *terminus a quo* of the cinematic narrative. That this is the case is obvious enough in the episode of the Appian Way whores that immediately follows the subway episode. But, as is clear in the first episode, Fellini's own narrative growth does not always coincide with the disclosure of cinematic narrative possibilities. This disjunction between Fellini's narrative growth and the narrative growth revealed by the camera continues to mark the story later, nowhere more than in the episode of the Appian Way whores, in which Fellini is entirely absent as either voice or image. The Appian Way whores episode and the cinematic possibilities opened up there will be discussed later in the chapter; for the moment the story to be considered is that of Fellini's own process of moving beyond archaic narrative habits to a cinematic relation to his world.

After the subway episode, then, Fellini's next appearance is at Marcello Mastroianni's house, located, significantly enough, as Fellini's voice-over says, "at the beginning of the Appian Way." Fellini is still trying to begin. He is still functioning under the Aristotelian narrative precept which dictates that all things must have a beginning "which is not itself necessarily after anything else."[11] With Fellini at the helm, the action accordingly continues its trip back into the narrative categories dictated by the classical mind, and recalling Fellini's own voice-over narration for the anti-image of G. Mastorna: "His voyage would have begun like this."

From his first appearance onscreen, Mastroianni clearly belongs to the bipolar black-and-white world of the early Fellini movies in which he starred. (In fact, the first woman with whom Mastroianni is seen wears a half-white, half-black robe and wig which directly associate the actor with the visually polarized.) Fellini has thus entered a world more decadent than that of the Mastorna set or than that of Genius's severed heads and ghosts: first, because he takes the story into the past of what is visually present in the action of *Director's Notebook* itself (that is, into *La dolce vita* and 8½) and can therefore be known only as a remembrance, which in effect devalues the ongoing narrative process; second, because at Mastroianni's house Fellini stubbornly seeks "inspiration" from a world-renowned professional actor as a substitute for the narrative potentialities he has already seen in the nameless, past-less images of the Colosseum, of the subway, and even of the Mastorna set; and third, because in so ascribing mastery to Mastroianni's image, Fellini implicitly places himself in a position of supremacy over it, thereby turning the creative process into a hierarchical structure: Fellini rules over the supreme image (Mastroianni) whose secretary, Cesarino ("little Caesar," the merely imperial), opens the door to Mastroianni's shrine and orders the film crew not to step on the grass, an order he gives by talking directly at the camera. The camera is again the lowest power in the narrative chain of being.

It is not at all surprising that this rigidly structured world of Mastroianni altogether fails to move. Mastroianni himself sums up the inertness of the world he inhabits when later in the episode he complains to Fellini, "You see, Federico, my friend, from now on I'm typecast—Latin lover." Mastroianni of course refers to the statement made by one of the gossip columnists who "casts" him when she tells him, "But you are the most famous Latin lover."

The fact is, however, that almost everyone surrounding Mastroianni typecasts him in one way or another. At all moments Mastroianni is *told* what he is. The very first question asked of him by a gossip columnist is, "What is the difference between a Latin woman and a northern woman?" Mastroianni fumbles for words and soon admits that he doesn't know. Yet Mastroianni's embrace of the woman in the black-and-white robe as he listens to the columnist suggests that he too lives in and through the divisive artifice expressed by the question of the columnist. "Would you say," the columnist continues, "that a Latin woman makes a better mother and a northern woman a better companion?" To these inane classifications, Mastroianni, the "principal image," replies, "Uh, yes." In relation to the gossip columnist, Mastroianni's entire function is to be verbally stereotyped as a man whose vast experiences with women allow him readily to discriminate among them. But implicit in the interviewer's question is the still more entrenched notion that the master image ought to have a "say," that he ought to be capable of intellectualizing.

A second gossip columnist asks Mastroianni, "What is the secret of your elegance?" Again he is baffled by the question, so the columnist supplies the answer: "The secret of your elegance is one word, simplicity." In a humorously ironic cut that shows the interviewer's stupidity, her answer coincides with the shot where Cesarino helps Mastroianni don the heavy full-length fur coat as Mastroianni continues to pose next to the model wearing the garish pink gown and the chandelierlike earrings. It is also worthy of note that one of the columnists earlier asks Mastroianni what ten books he would take with him on a desert island. He replies, cynically, that he would take a book of instructions on how to build a house and how to install a telephone. The gossip columnist, however, will not settle for the reply which, to her mind, clearly fails to show Mastroianni as a man of high intellect. So again she supplies the response: "But joking aside, wouldn't you decide on *Don Quixote, Moby Dick, Madame Bovary, War and Peace, Dead Souls, David Copperfield,* and the Bible?" And Mastroianni obligingly replies, "Oh, yes, sure, especially the Bible."

Beneath their surface frivolity, these questions have an old-narrative significance all their own. They ask "what." They thus attempt to elicit the essence or substance of the image: they seek to know what the image is like "in real life" and thus deny it a life of its own. (In this way, of course, there is little difference between the gossip columnists and the Fellini who asked Genius about the "real ancient Romans." Also, it is to be borne in mind that Fellini himself is here playing the role of an "insider" who documents the "real" life and lifestyle of Marcello Mastroianni.) Furthermore, since Mastroianni's image lacks any inherent narrative energies, it owes its existence to nothing but its passive capacity to absorb the essential qualities—elegant lover, intellectual, and so forth—that conform to the columnists' concepts of what a superior image should be. The image therefore loses its individuality and becomes instead an "identity"—contrived and reduced to conform to the public ideal of just such an identity. In short, the secret of Mastroianni's image is the extraneously imposed and ever-reductive word.

Along with his introduction of Mastroianni as a "Roman" with "all the virtues" and "all the vices" that befit "a true Roman," Fellini himself contributes to the typecasting of Mastroianni's image when he implicitly orders the camera to see as though it were a still camera, or, as in the subway sequence, a recorder. Thus, not coincidentally, the first image of this episode is a tight shot of Cesarino's mouth. Or else the camera gazes at the gossip columnists when they ask their questions and cuts to Mastroianni when he is supposed to answer them. The camera also cuts from Mastroianni's immobile image to the photographers themselves, thus identifying itself (or, more precisely, being forced by Fellini to identify itself) with their still cameras. Mastroianni is also typecast, then, by the publicity photographers themselves. And what is worse, the photographers do not tell him what to say, but what to do: "Marcello, . . . would you put on the fur coat now, please?" or "Marcello, the hat now," or "Can you change your coat now?" All these orders are for Mastroianni to put on more weight; they are intended to conceal rather than reveal the image (especially so in contrast to the only vitally active image in this episode, Marina Boratto, who, in a bikini, casually dashes by Mastroianni and jumps headfirst into the swimming pool). Mastroianni's black suit and hat further single him out as an abstraction from the world of color.[12] And even his face is "cast" into a particularly abstract mold when one of the photographers asks Mastroianni to assume a "virile" expression, but with "timidity." Mastroianni is typecast by the frozen frame of the still camera. He thus acquires a narrative affinity with the initial image of Genius. But whereas the frozen image of Genius at least breaks into talk, Mastroianni's resides in a narrative limbo; that is, he lacks cinematic energies and cannot even talk back. He is altogether the product of artifice; or conversely, he is a deified image only to those "outsiders" who see the finished product of the masters of artifice. Mastroianni is right to a certain extent—he is "typecast," but he is typecast not only as a Latin lover, but as whatever type his thoroughly abused image will allow him to play.

Toward the end of the episode the camera looks at Mastroianni as

he ceremoniously acknowledges the hysterical adoration of the bus-
load of fanatical women, themselves looking up at Mastroianni from
behind the barred bus windows, and thus reaffirming the artificially
deified status of Mastroianni's master image which the camera is
forced to see. At this moment the camera looks at Mastroianni's back
(as it did earlier at G. Mastorna's), and Fellini's voice reemerges, to
show his persistent will to dominate over the image, and to reaffirm
his commitment to the old narrative. "I thought of him," Fellini
says, "for the part of Mastorna. I had looked everywhere for this
character." With the creative eye persistently denied its expressive
zest, its energies have again been turned into the thinking, speaking, narrative forces of an ego that wills to create from a "part"
rather than from the whole, and that "had looked" but to see an
abstraction, a name.

Not surprisingly, the action now finds itself once more in an
artificial setting. During the greater portion of the screen-test episode, Mastroianni sits on a chair making strident noises on the cello
while a dozen attendants move slowly around him. They brush his
suit, wipe his brow, clear his eyes with collyrium, and so forth.
Through Fellini's "thought," Mastroianni becomes the center of
attention. Yet there has been no qualitative growth: there has been
no growth from an immanent creative center (Mastroianni is still the
image submitted to extraneous modifications, such as the hat, the
false mustache, and the cello which he obviously can't play); and he
is still immobile (he sits on the chair while all the satellite figures,
including Fellini and the camera, continue to revolve around him).

Suddenly the attendants disappear and the camera stops circling
around Mastroianni. Fellini stops coaxing, dictating, and now affirms his freedom from archaic narrative sources when he says, "I
felt [G. Mastorna] was not there." Now the "I" feels rather than
thinks. And now Fellini sees the urge to control the image for what
it is, "a fool's dream," to use the hippie poet's phrase.

But then Mastroianni rebels against Fellini's incipient vision of
the new narrative mode and invokes the past in an effort to save
himself from being totally abandoned by the reborn imagination.
"All right," Mastroianni says, "I understand. But when you made
La dolce vita wasn't I your character? In 8½ wasn't I right?" In his
very first verbal expression beyond the frivolity that he is made to
spout at his house, Mastroianni articulates the progress of Fellini's

imaginative incursion into the vision of new narrative values. For
Mastroianni *was* indeed a character, a central image who, alone and
fashioned out of an archaic imagination, became the vehicle for the
mere projection of an archetypal "Image of Man," and who, through
a capacity to act dramatically (which amounts to no more than a
capacity to absorb words as well as extraneous verbal dictates),
pretentiously became, as did all archaic characters, the measure of
all things, at the expense of the narrative powers of life itself.

"Yes, Marcello, I know," replies Fellini, "but those were other
films, different characters." Fellini is now also aware of *differences*
(as opposed to similarities between, say, subway and catacombs).
And his acknowledgment of "differences" begins with an affirmation, with a "yes." But Mastroianni in turn resorts to preying on
Fellini's sense of guilt, retorting, "No, Federico, it's because now
you have no faith. It's as if you're scared. If you could believe that I
am Mastorna, I would automatically become Mastorna." Fellini is
supposed to feel the full brunt of the sin that involves abandoning
the conventional narrative methods as exclusive sources for creation. In the prop room earlier, referring to his failure to make "The
Voyage of G. Mastorna," Fellini has said to the English-speaking
interviewer/narrator, "It gives [me] a kind of remorse, as if a million
eyes were staring at me, waiting." Through his archetypal identity,
his universal conscience, and his seductive ethical reprimands, Mastroianni would gladly have Fellini relive that early guilt. Certainly
Mastroianni is partially correct when he imputes to Fellini the failure to cast him as G. Mastorna. But just as certainly he cannot see
that Fellini's fortunate failure entails an awareness of the futility of
creating within an intellectual hierarchy, within the inhibitive confines of the will, of the ego, of the past. Even as he removes only one
side of the false mustache before the mirror, Mastroianni cannot see
that he remains in the world of artifice while Fellini, no longer
feeling the need to engage in polemics (to reply to Mastroianni's
"no"), moves on to explore his incipient vision of differences.

Now Fellini is free—free to create a new vision of the world; yet
more: in the process he is just as free to be created by it, to explore
and enjoy the supreme virtue of his embryonic vision, namely, his
own individual union with and continuous transition into the
pluralistic universe of images. At last, Fellini might well be saying,
along with Wallace Stevens:

The world is no longer an extraneous object, full of other extraneous objects, but an image. In the last analysis, it is with this image of the world that we are vitally concerned. We should not say, however, that the chief object of the imagination is to produce such an image. Among so many objects, it would be the merest improvisation to say of one, even though it is one with which we are vitally concerned, that it is the chief. The next step would be to assert that a particular image was the chief image. Again, it would be the merest improvisation to say of any image of the world, even though it was an image with which a vast accumulation of imaginations had been content, that it was the chief image. The imagination itself would not remain content with it nor allow us to do so. It is the irrepressible revolutionist.[13]

Henceforth the narrative activity of *Director's Notebook* involves, above all else, the vision—the revolutionary moral vision—of value in every individual image. Individual common images are the boundless source of narration for Fellini's revitalized imagination. Fellini's narrative acts have so far been mere archaic improvisations, hero-centered narrative sketches that have tentatively sought to reestablish the supremacy of an archetype or Transcendental Ego, and by extension, the value of otherworldliness that such hero-centered narratives have always exemplified. The accumulation of Fellini's narrative deeds up to the screen-test sequence have exhibited the fact that the importance—the value—of the image is directly derived from the image's past and from its socially or intellectually acquired status. It is this *identity* of the image that has so far in *Director's Notebook* created the chief image. The role imposed on the image has alone accounted for mastery, supremacy, dominance. Status, or identity, has thus been the only measure of value.

But after he abandons Mastroianni's image, Fellini begins to rebel creatively against that narrative which has in essence preoccupied (and contented) the vast accumulation of imaginations in the Western narrative tradition. Now, however, the common image, which is to say *any* image, is the chief image—not because it is endowed with otherworldliness so it may rule over the world, but because its very presence onscreen constitutes its importance as a union of fact and value, an importance beyond rational justification, beyond names, roles, and identities. The chief image, in fine, ceases to be chief because of its "aristocratic" origin, and becomes, in its discrete and fleeting existence, the chief by virtue of the importance

of its contribution to the making of a new narrative. The importance
of the common images, their "supremacy," depends on the value
that Fellini can envision in their visual existence itself, and, recip-
rocally, in the value that they themselves can make Fellini see. This
is the birth not only of the democratic image, but of the democratic
imagination as well. No matter how fleeting their appearances onscreen, the common images will become the enduring source of narration, expressing an enduring world of values—a world of ideal
actions—out of their finite existences as new narrative facts. And
should divinity succeed, as it no doubt can, in making itself manifest
in these individual common images, then it will be all the more
glorious precisely for having appeared in just such a form.

That Fellini grows further into a vision of perfect reciprocity
between the seeing and the seen is perhaps best summed up by
himself late in the casting office episode, near the end of *Director's
Notebook.* He says: "Yes, I know, it might seem cynical, cruel. But
no, I am very fond of all these characters who are always chasing
after me, following me from one film to another. They are all a little
mad, I know that. They say they need me, but the truth is that I
need them more. Their human qualities are rich, comic, and sometimes very moving."

Here, where he has seen scores of hopefuls who have come to see
him, Fellini expresses his newly discovered vision of the wisdom of
the common image—of the images which, like those at the end of
the subway ride, are nameless and yet abound with individuality.
Fellini, it must be borne in mind, is present in this episode as a
camera eye. But his presence is also determined by his hands, seen
throughout the episode behind his side of the desk. He is thus
aligned with the camera in a way that has not happened earlier,
where, as at the Colosseum, images addressed the camera when
talking to the Fellini voice and as a result created a doubt as to
whether Fellini was indeed the camera eye.

At the casting office, the camera takes in the words of the hopefuls. But unlike Genius's or the professor's words, theirs do not seek
to dominate over creative vision. Rather, they reveal their passion
to express themselves to the creative eye in their own discrete ways.
The "characters" do not sit, they "chase"; they move and find their
way into an esthetic event ("a film"). And as they move physically,

so obviously do they move spiritually, imaginatively—beckoning to the creative eye that it may nourish itself on their richness.

But Fellini himself is not quite as quick as the camera eye was when it rebelled against narrative "nonbeing" and beheld the new images in the subway. Fellini's realization of the potentialities of the cinematic narrative come late in the story. Yet far from implying inadequacy on his part, Fellini's difficulty in assenting to the readiness of the camera eye to reveal novelty is in fact a more complete triumph than the elusive victory enjoyed by the camera in the subway. The narrative genius of *Director's Notebook* lies in its creative capacity to incorporate and grow from rather than to reject outright the archaic narrative values. The genuine narrative breakthrough is the unified vision of opposites which consolidates the competing narrative energies and extends them into an altogether new dimension.

As an example of the inherence of the new in the old, consider the Colosseum episode. From the Mastorna prop room, the action cuts to Fellini's voice-over narration as it announces that the story is about to undertake "another voyage, a voyage in time." Then the English-speaking interviewer/narrator takes over the verbal narration. This narrator is never seen, so that he is more of a narrative atavism even than the Fellini who talks over the Mastorna set, if only because in that early episode Fellini has already become an image and the English speaker is never more than a voice. Also of course he speaks his native English, that language with which Fellini himself has so much difficulty but nevertheless forces upon a number of the participants in the story (the woman with the powder at the Colosseum, Giulietta Masina, Genius, and Mastroianni).

The English speaker says: "The Colosseum. In this half-world of Rome in the small hours, Fellini is studying the night wanderers, looking for parallels between modern Rome and Nero's Rome. Fellini's new film is partially based on the *Satyricon*, a Roman novel of the first century." The first thing to notice about his verbal narration is that it viciously assumes that Fellini's "voyage in time" is necessarily a voyage into the past. Nowhere in the preceding episodes has Fellini referred to time as the past. This narrator—thoroughly intellectual—thinks there can be time without events. Moreover, to anticipate, as does the English-speaking narrator, that this "new

film" is *Fellini-Satyricon* requires that the action of the present be
robbed of its intrinsic value. And more: nowhere in the preceding
episodes—or for that matter in subsequent ones—does Fellini himself refer any action in *Director's Notebook* either to Petronius's
Satyricon or to a movie "partially based" on that novel. The English
narrator therefore ascribes an intention to Fellini's search. The narrative act is burdened by a teleology; the present, according to the
English narrator, is but a means to a fixed end. Thus he implicitly
slurs over the process of narrative realization taking place right
under his intellectual nose. And thus also he acquires the character
of that most mischievous personage of conventional narrative, the
"unreliable narrator." If only for this reason, it is dangerous to believe the English-speaking narrator when he says that one of the
men has threatened to call the police if Fellini and his crew do not
leave the Colosseum.

For this narrator is intellectually disturbed by the "atmosphere"
into which Fellini's imaginative adventure has brought him. He
speaks of the Colosseum's "half-world," of its nocturnal inhabitants
and "shadowy individuals," and of the atmosphere itself as "a little
unnerving, with shadows flitting at every corner." But the greater,
namely, the visual, fact is that many of the men and women the
camera sees at the Colosseum prove the narrator's fears totally un-
founded. For example, the "woman with the powder" quite
willingly explains to Fellini that she puts dust from the Colosseum
into envelopes and sells it to American tourists who use it as a cure
for rheumatism. One of the men is quite willing to let the camera
get close to him, and he combs his hair in front of it, almost as if he
were using the camera as a mirror. When the camera focuses on a
group of women and transvestites, one of the women, the short-
haired one, shyly turns her face away from it; then, turning around
and seeing that the camera is still on her, she smiles coquettishly at
it. The camera sees all of the nameless faces, revealing their individuality, their innocence as images to which only an uneasy intellect such as the narrator's would ascribe socially and ethically
undesirable characteristics.

Thus what is markedly different in this earlier episode from those
later ones already examined is, first, that here Fellini is not verbally
narrating. He talks to the images, not at them or about them. Second, he is not willfully searching for "the real ancient" past. In other

words, since in the Colosseum episode he is not present as an image that narrates with intellectual purpose, his narrative affinities lie with the camera eye and not with the English speaker, who now in effect assumes the narrative function that Fellini performed during the first episode. In fact, Fellini's relation to the images of the Colosseum is not unlike his relation to those at the casting office, the basic difference, of course, being that at the Colosseum, Fellini "chases" after the images whereas in the casting office they chase after him.

What it is crucial to elicit from the Colosseum episode is that, like the Mastorna episode, it interweaves the components of the cinematic with those of the conventional narrative. Yet at the Colosseum the images of men and women do not lie down to die, as they do at Mastorna; nor do they recite decadent poems for the camera. The images go to meet each other, to form relations; and the eye, not the word, confirms those relations as concrete, individual connections—connections from which the camera itself cannot be ultimately disassociated, but in the interpretation of which the words of the English narrator are not only superfluous but clearly misleading. In this way, the Colosseum episode is one more possible model for Fellini's own narrative growth. For here, as in the casting office, he is united to and identified with the visual powers that witness the creative possibilities of the common image.

Shortly after the Colosseum episode, when Fellini expresses his weariness of wandering "from ruin to ruin like this," he announces, for the first time in the movie, that "different feeling" which his voice-over later expresses as he abandons the Mastroianni/Mastorna project.

Furthermore, by cutting away from the episode that follows—the "deleted" sequence from *Nights of Cabiria*—the action frees itself from Giulietta Masina's divisive verbal narration in that sequence. For other than Fellini himself, Masina is the first "chief image" in *Director's Notebook*. And like a good chief image Masina has the function of recalling the past. As Fellini wanted the professor to do, Masina talks to the camera. Hence the camera for the first time is a recording device when Masina asks it: "Do you remember that picture *The Nights of Cabiria*?" Thus not only does the action cut away from the present (the Colosseum) to the past (the deleted sequence from *Cabiria* via the Masina interview) and from the common images to the dominant image, but it also finds itself looking at a black-and-white rather than at a color world. And thus the potentially creative eye of the camera is intimidated by its first venture outside the world of artifice, that is, into the Colosseum. It is as if, meekly submitting to the pronouncement of one of the night wanderers at the Colosseum who tells Fellini that "the characters he seeks belong to a world of fiction," the camera is forced to return to artifice—that is, to the safety of an imaginative feat accomplished through the agency of a chief image. Art and life (*Cabiria* and the life around the Colosseum) accordingly become mutually exclusive events.

But by cutting away from Cabiria and "the man with the sack," the narrative powers free themselves from the hulk of an isolated snippet of narration that does not even belong to the unity of that "remembered" narrative feat, *Nights of Cabiria*. The deleted *Cabiria* sequence is as much a ruin as Mastorna or even as the Colosseum, whose last image, the man with the sack, is itself burdened, physically as well as by humanitarian commitments.

From the black-and-white world of the deleted *Cabiria* sequence, the action cuts to a brief shot of the Colosseum and then to a long, high-angle shot of Rome that precedes the voice-over narration. "My old Romans," Fellini says, "are still those I saw when I was a little boy and first went to the movies." The voice doesn't talk against the image. In fact, this is the first episode where there is more than a conflicting presence of archaic and cinematic narrative modes. Here both modes contribute actively to generate the narrative advance of *Director's Notebook* itself, as well as to extend Fellini's own narrative growth.

The action cross-cuts from the movie of the "old Romans" to the activities of the moviegoers, some of whom, like the man and woman in the right foreground, look up to the screen as if entranced, while the heavyset usher picks up a kicking, screaming child and sets him on his chair; others fight for front-row seats; and boys scream and slap each other. The viewers, in short, are a cinematic narration all their own. In this world where the seeing and the seen are now actively united in a world of color, the polarities of previous (and of some subsequent) episodes are altogether absent.

Moreover, the past, which when seen in relation to the dominant images and adventitious authorities is a retreat from the visual particulars, here turns out to involve an experience of concrete and individual relations in which the visual energies participate fully. The past is rescued, as it were, by its novel relation to cinematic values. The possibility of a reciprocal relation between image and camera, the seeing and the seen, is established by the tendency of the "old Romans" in the movie of Fellini's youth to aim their actions at the camera (and thus by extension at the theatergoers and at the viewers of *Director's Notebook*). The perfidious mistress looks straight into the camera as she flexes her clawlike hands and assumes an expression of extreme villainy. The murder of the emperor takes place in front of the camera. And when the emperor is stabbed, he gazes at the camera with a look more of surprise and resignation than of pained betrayal.

The movie of the "old Romans," purely visual, is for the camera, for the eye, not for the intellect. And the movie moves. The would-be assassins chase the emperor around the palace at the speeded-up pace of early silent movies; and at the end all the conspirators cheerfully carry the empress on their shoulders. Unlike the deleted *Cabiria* sequence, this action is not burdened by sentimental humanitarianism. Nor is the action made to carry the weight of an intellectual hankering, such as Cabiria's, after the identity of the man with the sack. No doubt the stilted, "emoted" actions of the images, the confining theater stage, and the movie's own theme of imperial power make the silent movie of Fellini's youth incapable of fully revealing the potentialities of the new narrative. But what is important to note is the way the whole sequence begins to move toward a cinematic redemption of an archaic value like "the past." The past in this sequence—the youth that Fellini claims to remember—is in fact *imagined*. For unlike the divisive, black-and-white, literally accurate memory of Masina, (as presented in the unused *Cabiria* sequence), Fellini's youth, including the silent movie, is in color. The movie is consequently an event that could not have taken place in the chronological past of Fellini's youth. Yet far more crucial than mere chronology is the fact that Fellini's imagination transforms the narrative commitment of *Director's Notebook*—transforms, that is, the relation between the narrator and the narrated—in a way in which Masina cannot significantly change *Nights of Cabiria.* In this way, then, Fellini's imagined "youth" contains the seeds for growth into the vision of images of the present such as those he much later encounters in the slaughterhouse episode. At the slaughterhouse the images that act, that create the action, are not characters endowed with special qualities of inherited nobility but common images of life itself. The narrative advance inherent in the contrast between the Masina narration and the movie of Fellini's youth therefore announces a process of growth from "youth" to "maturity," just as, eventually, the contrast between the movie of Fellini's youth and the slaughterhouse episode marks a continuation of the process from the "old" and the staged to the vision of the new, uncontrolled narrative of the slaughterhouse. The perfidious mistress of the movie thus readily becomes the shy woman in red at the slaughterhouse—released from the confining stage yet retaining all of the harmless, comic cruelty of her "ancient" and "noble" counterpart.

Even more crucial to the growth of cinematic narrative energies in the whole episode is its very last image. A boy in a blue sailor suit sits on the lap of an old man. Both look at the screen with fascination. They see the images and they are images. The embodiments of the old and the new acquire an intrinsic unity by virtue of the narrative process which they witness but which they also constitute. Thus the last image is no mere passive symbol of the reconciliation of opposites. The seeing sees and is seen in one indivisible act. Life *does* as art, art as life: the meeting ground is the action in the ever-unfolding present.

In terms of the structural arrangement of *Director's Notebook,* the old-movie sequence is also a model for the Appian Way episode, an episode which also discloses the growth of the narrative model where the archaic and the cinematic coexist. It too begins with a verbal narration by an unseen speaker. The speaker, however, is Marina Boratto, and she introduces the episode with a descriptive accuracy unmatched by Fellini or by any other verbal narrator in the story. "Here," she says, "among the tombs and phantoms of the past, there are also creatures of flesh and blood. If you use a little imagination, these girls are easily transformed into their ancient counterparts." In contrast to Fellini's narration or to Genius's or to the professor's, this speech makes explicit reference to the present ("here"). Also, the "phantoms" that so disturbed the sensibility of the English-speaking narrator readily become "creatures of flesh and blood." And Marina makes an unabashed appeal to the imagination. It is the imagination which, for one thing, clarifies and unifies the categories of time that remained polarized in Fellini's introduction to his "old Romans." But most important is the fact that there is no longer an exclusive possession of narrative powers, as though they were the "faculty" of a privileged being, such as Fellini, Masina, Genius, or the professor. That is, whereas Fellini calls the images on the screen "*my* old Romans," Marina says, "if *you* use a little imagination." This "underling" Fellini has introduced as "my script girl" thus indicates that the imagination belongs to all—to Marina, to the participants in the action, and to the viewer of *Director's Notebook*. We are now the active audience. We have been asked to participate in the action in a way analogous to the way the audience of Fellini's youth participated.

On the field next to the road, a small fire burns. Four modern Roman women stroll the field. Before the camera cuts to the vivid red truck in which the four modern Roman men arrive, the women have already been transformed into "their ancient counterparts." Cutting back to the field, the camera sees the woman in the red Roman toga charge at it as she grimaces threateningly. But unlike the perfidious empress of Fellini's old Roman movie, this woman kills no one. (In fact, she will soon enough make love to one of the men.) The camera then cuts again to the four men, who stand in a row beside the truck, their backs to it, looking in the direction of the field. Then one of the men looks quickly to his right and is surprised to see, as does the camera, that one of his companions, the small, slender one, has turned into a Roman legionnaire. When the camera turns to the other three men, they too are dressed as legionnaires. The surprise of the truck driver at the transformation of his friend is brief. It is not, as it was in the professor's case, a cause for intellectual distress, a reason for wanting to get off the train. Whereas the professor's encounter with the image results in a withdrawal from the visual, the men on the truck rush to the field to make love to images. Furthermore, since there are no words to explain the transformation, it is clear that the camera acts as the extension of a collective imagination. Through the camera, which is now none other than the imagination itself, there is a newborn capacity directly to confirm and to follow the immanent transitions of the images. The imagination is, moreover, free to create an immanent order, an order that visually reveals, to disturbed intellects such as the professor's, that, as Bergson taught, "disorder is simply the order we are not looking for."[14]

The four men charge into the field and comically, clumsily, enact the life of sexually starved legionnaires. Here the action continues to exist for the delight of the creative eye, especially when one of the men interrupts his lovemaking and, turning from the woman, looks straight at the camera and winks at it.

At the end of this episode, when the men, still wearing their legionnaire uniforms, leave in the truck, much more has happened than an arbitrarily staged union of past and present. The event is itself; and to describe it by means of temporal labels involves the superfluous imposition of a mediating intellect upon the immediate act. The camera and our imaginations confirm the creative advance in this episode: we have ourselves become imaginative participants in a world where images imagine their own possibilities for change.

When Fellini goes from the Mastroianni/Mastorna screen-test to the slaughterhouse, he actively searches for the "new film," which grows not only out of the death of the Mastorna project but, at least by implication, from the model for narrative possibilities inherent in the Appian Way episode as well. The initial import of the action's transition to the slaughterhouse is that Fellini doesn't use words to reject the old narrative mode. That is, the story is now beyond dialectics because there is no dominant conceptual mode of thought dictating its transitions. To illustrate by comparing a previous juxtaposition of episodes, there is now no Fellini voice-over which rejects the "ruins" (as "thesis") and deliberately ventures into the movies of his youth (as "antithesis").

But in spite of the self-generated transition to the common images of the slaughterhouse, the episode is again burdened by a mediator between the action on the screen and the action of the imaginative viewer. There is little to say about the perverse function of the English-speaking narrator that has not been said in the section that deals with Fellini's visit to the Colosseum. He again displays his penchant to reduce the visual action to verbal abstraction. He again imputes an intention to Fellini ("Fellini wanted to track down . . .").

And he again ignores differences (since he sees the trip to the slaughterhouse as an attempt to evoke the ancient). But precisely because he steadfastly adheres to his intellectual narration, he creates a narrative contrast that illuminates the difference in which Fellini's own words now operate in *Director's Notebook.*

Early in the slaughterhouse episode, the English-speaking narrator tells of Fellini's search for the "ferocious" and "bloodthirsty" aspects of the world. But later, when the two butchers in gladiator costumes stop fighting because one of them suffers a small scratch on the ear, Fellini's voice-over says, "Do you know what has happened? . . . The great gladiator is ready to cry like a baby." Words function on behalf of the cinematic narrative energies when they operate descriptively, as do Fellini's. On the other hand, they function to repress those same energies when they operate demonstratively, interpretively, as do the English-speaking narrator's.

At the slaughterhouse, the narrative advance is the direct result of the actions of the creative eye with which Fellini himself comes to be fully aligned roughly halfway through the episode. Consider the camera's activity as it enters the slaughterhouse. The first shot is almost dark, but the camera soon finds a square of light. The camera continues to move along a fence until it finds an entrance. Then it moves into the building. A door opens and in the dim light the camera sees the bare butchering tables. It moves alongside them until it discovers the motionless silhouettes of a group of men, some sitting on the tables, some standing by them. Now with more light, the camera sees the men's images as they goad the pigs in a pen, and soon it sees the dead pigs dangling from the conveyor system. Suddenly, there is a sound of martial drums. The action has suddenly cut away to the white stone busts of ancient Romans, which appear on the screen one at a time. In a totally dark background each one moves swiftly, as if floating. Some move toward the camera, some move from it and then disappear, giving way to others. Then, just as abruptly, this series ends and the camera is looking at the heads of burly, heavyset men out in the light of day.

The creative eye extends its narrative possibilities through a process of discovering the very source of vision, the light. The process involves the illumination of the obscure (the silhouettes as well as the dark stone busts) and the mobility of the motionless (the men outside the slaughterhouse and the moving busts). And the process also reveals the camera's own affinity to "creatures of flesh and blood." Yet it must be borne in mind that the camera moves from the dark inside to the light outside through the agency of art in the form of the stone busts, even if these are associated with the art of the past. That is, the stone busts do not function as structural recapitulations of the severed heads in the prop room or at the cemetery. They move toward the light; they are alive. There is accordingly no rejection of any art form. Instead art, the art of the stone heads, begets life—the living heads of the burly Roman butchers outside the slaughterhouse.

The camera delights in inseparable unions between art and life at the slaughterhouse. The men become gladiators, Roman senators, or emperors. Or the shy woman, for instance, becomes the cruel spectator in red Roman toga cheering for her favorite gladiator. The image of the shy woman serves in turn as a model that illustrates Fellini's own alignment with, indeed his present inseparability from, the eye's power to discover the narrative possibilities of the image. Caterina Boratto, a former chief image herself (in 8½ and especially in *Juliet of the Spirits*), says to Fellini that once in the slaughterhouse she saw the animals being killed and swore that she would never eat meat again. "But," Fellini replies, "I detect a gleam of cruelty in your eyes, . . . I think, Caterina, that you will be perfect in a part of a woman of great ferocity and terrifying sadism."

Almost immediately, Caterina becomes the image of Fellini's detection. Like her nameless counterpart, she too gestures passionately, almost orgasmically delighting in the gladiatorial combat. The great actress is now no better than a common woman from the slaughterhouse. The "different feeling" that Fellini had toward the dominant image at the end of the Mastroianni/Mastorna screentest is actualized in terms of the transformation of a once-dominant image into its possibilities as just another image, as the chief image only within a given instance which is within neither Caterina's nor Fellini's power to perpetuate.

By a continuing process of narrative concrescence, the slaughterhouse episode is a model for the narrative discoveries at the casting office sequence. And at the casting office the images imagine Fellini as the imaginative power that narrates their lives. This is the subtlest narrative advance of *Director's Notebook: the*

image which imagines is also imagined. Thus in the very last scene of
Director's Notebook, when Fellini is once again an image (as he is
not, in the casting office), he is silent, now seeing his own and the
camera's image in the make-up mirror, now showing a Roman how
to gesture, now looking through the viewfinder as four young men
in Roman garb walk up to the camera in single file and walk offscreen. Fellini is both image and creative eye, seeing what sees
back, creating what creates him.

But the subtlety of this narrative dimension that entails a perfect
narrative reciprocity between the creative individual and the creative world begins at the casting office. Perhaps nowhere in this
sequence is the narrative reciprocity so explicit as in the scene
where the bald man humbly says to Fellini that if he (the man) had a
wig that looked like Elvis Presley's hair, it would change his whole
life. In his own unassuming way, he is among the first to announce
the fact that change is not merely a quantitative factor, much less an
illusion, but that it is a spiritual passion, indeed the fundamental
human need. The bald man therefore proclaims that he can imagine
for Fellini, that he can see Fellini as the creator of change. As the
man's vision suggests, images do not play roles; they are not "cast";
rather, they become *decharacterized,* they become the things
themselves, the immanent narrative potentialities of which instruct
Fellini in the ways of transforming the image organically by changing it visually.

It is, however, equally crucial to the narrative import of the
casting room episode to see that each of its discrete units (that is,
each individual's relation to the creative eye) contributes equally to
the further exploration and unification of new narrative terrain. It is
impossible to attend to all of them, so great is their variety; a few
examples will have to suffice to illustrate the narrative unity of the
episode. There is an actor in the office. He is, in the words of the
narrator with the Italian accent,[15] "a professional actor," and he is
there to recite a poem from Chekhov, "Man Alone." Although he is
the bearer of the archaic narrative powers, he is not burdened by
"stardom," as are Mastroianni and Masina. On the other hand, the
poem's title itself singles him out as the image of man lacking the
capacity to imagine himself in a world of living relations. Yet later in
the episode, long after he is through reciting, this actor, a thin,
weak-looking type, looks in awe at the Roman matron's two sons,

whom she brings to Fellini that he may cast them in the roles of
Romulus and Remus. The actor is not like the hippie poet who
ended his words and lay down to die. Finished with words without
having to reject them, he now becomes a participant in the world of
images, seeing and partaking of their vitality. The purely spiritual
(the poet) and the purely physical (the sons) unite within a single
scene and are accordingly transformed into the genuinely new narrative possibility.

Also, Fellini's penchant for possession (as seen repeatedly in his
earlier references to Marina as "my script girl," to "my old Romans," and to "my film"), disappears for good when he refuses even
to consider buying a painting from the con-artist who says he has
acquired a work by a painter "more important than Raphael." The
man offers Fellini an abstractly conjured figure, offers him, in short,
"high art," and he is the only one who is virtually thrown out of the
office. Fellini is no longer the man who readily takes to the past as
the most valued possession. He no longer values the past for itself,
that is, in the way he did by preserving the prop room for "The
Voyage of G. Mastorna," or for that matter as he did in his nostalgic
attachments to the movies of his youth and to Mastroianni.

And Fellini also rejects the intellectualism of the woman who
asks his opinion about whether or not women should be virgins. The
question is not unlike that posed to Mastroianni by one of the gossip
columnists regarding the differences between Latin and northern
women, but in addition, the woman's question demands the sort of
self-reflective response that Mastroianni himself demanded of Fellini at the end of the screen-test sequence. Fellini, however, doesn't
reply to the woman's question. As he was beyond self-justification
when he cut away from Mastroianni's accusations and to the
slaughterhouse, so is he now beyond the need to intellectualize out
of an abstraction such as "womanhood" or "virginity." Fellini does
not indulge in intellectual negation. He merely ignores the woman's
question and gets on with the task of seeing.

Still another vital function of the human images that come to see
and be seen by Fellini is to confirm his incipient narrative wisdom in
those previous episodes where his free imagination had led him,
however briefly and inconclusively, to venture into new narrative
combinations. The very first hopeful at the casting office, a woman
who is a poet, so Marina says, tells Fellini that he will never make a

good movie "if he goes on using the same dreary old faces." More than a repetition of Fellini's search for the "right faces" during the slaughterhouse episode, what happens at this moment is that Marina now narrates about a narrator (the poet) who in turn narrates (tells Fellini) about a new mode of making a story. She is as aware as Fellini now is of the possibility of extending man's narrative powers by making fresh visual connections with a new face, such as hers, for instance. The poet also has that "different feeling," that passion to undertake "a new voyage."

Another example of the narrative wisdom of the common image is evident in the old woman, the "dressmaker" who stumbles into the office. She feels, Marina says, that it is her duty "to make an audience happy after a hard day's work." Then the dressmaker hands Fellini a photograph of herself as a child. The connection that Fellini made with the Romans of his youth is clearly paralleled by this woman who, through the image of her own youth, introduces her own vision of a unity between past and present. She is clearly a counterpart of the last image in the movie-of-the-youth episode (the old man with the boy on his lap). But more, she is the union of old and young come to rescue Fellini's early vision of his youth from its purely private, isolated state.

Like the old dressmaker, the voluptuous blonde who is "not officially an actress" (having only played Joan of Arc twice in Sunday school) comes to see and be seen. Also like the dressmaker, she has no clearly defined sense of what she wants to be in Fellini's movie. Yet the unofficial image (literally the image without a professed role), becomes the object of visual and imaginative attention precisely because she is the unofficial image. The intrinsic value resides in the visual act of the camera commingling with her passion to participate in a narrative event for its own sake. What matters now above everything else is "this communion which is created . . . between you and a face."[16] Actress or not, official or unofficial, the woman participates in and contributes to the making of a story. The child actress has matured into a cinematic image, just as both Fellini and *Director's Notebook* mature narratively and continue to do so.

And neither does the other, still more voluptuous blonde, possess any theatrical talents. She tells Fellini that she speaks fluent Arabic and cooks well, obviously not talents that are highly regarded by conventional directors, but which again indicate that the image

itself possesses its own talents. And then she unhesitatingly tells
Fellini, "Anyway, I think you need me." Rather than hark back to
the movie's own past, as do the poet, the dressmaker, and the first
blonde, this woman anticipates Fellini's realization of his "need" for
these "characters," of the thoroughly human and moral need to see
and be seen. In contrast to the once all-important theatrical ability
of the image, it is now the "human qualities" that are valued above
all else—their qualities to liberate the spirit from the onus of the
past and from the search for an essential image, but also the qualities
that allow the spirit to create a new vision of the image as a narrative
phenomenon, of each particular image as both the world and its
narrator.

Perhaps the image that most successfully displays capacities to
proclaim affinities with extensive and unifying narrative possibilities
is the woman with the accordion. She says to Fellini, "Your films
express exactly the same things as my music." What is in question
throughout the woman's ensuing performance and eventual completion of her song ("Fortune, Where Art Thou?") is not whether her
music expresses "exactly" the same "things" as do Fellini's movies,
but whether by the time she completes her song, Fellini's irritation
and his reluctance to listen to her have not in fact been transformed
into a fascination with the narrative possibilities of this woman's
image. And indeed, because she so successfully captures Fellini's
imagination, the camera eventually moves closer to her, thus enacting its own passion to discover the woman's capacity not only to
express herself, not only to contribute to the creation of the "film,"
but also to unify the inside of the office with the hall outside where
the dozens of hopefuls wait.

As she sings, the camera cuts from her face to the faces of other
hopefuls and then to the hall. It sees the midget in the background,
pans left, seeing all of the images that have been in the room, and
settles on the little girl in the foreground, on the new image, who
looks smilingly at the camera as she sways to the rhythm of the
accordion music. Not only does the woman interest Fellini in her
artistic "expression"; not only does she lead him into a unified vision
of all the images he has seen; she also unites Fellini's creative eye
with the world of images.

By the time the camera returns to the office, where Fellini now
articulates his "need" for "these characters," the narrative import of

Director's Notebook is totally disclosed by virtue of its capacities to grow as a union of contrasting narrative modes. Fellini does not make the movie he "prefers the most." The one that prefers him the most is the one he assents to.

From the background of the now-empty hall, a giant walks up close to the camera, and looking straight into it asks, "Good morning, Signor Fellini, any work for me in your new film?" Fellini, once the man of the will, has unquestionably grown into an indivisible union with the narrative powers of the image. And the giant, announcing a new day, *has* found "work" in the new film. His work is to confirm the creative evolution of narrative powers through the agency of his own discrete act before the creative eye.

That the next scene in *Director's Notebook* is recognizably the staging for the opening shots of *Fellini-Satyricon* in no way robs *Director's Notebook* of its own narrative achievement. Quite the contrary, in fact. For the transition into a new event is living proof of the extensive narrative energies discovered throughout its action. The new narrative discovery makes of *Director's Notebook* the perfectly incomplete event—"perfect" because of its organic indivisibility, "incomplete" because it begets more art, more life. In this way *Director's Notebook* is a narrative value in itself, its contrasting narrative modes and its varieties of relations to the image of man displaying the new unity of its self-organizing feat in as valuable a way as that in which the creative transitions of life itself are made.

2

The Narrative Dilemma

SEVEN BEAUTIES

At the first sight
They have changed eyes.
....
Thy eyes are almost set in thy head.
THE TEMPEST, act 1, act 3

By one of those rare, timely miracles of the imagination which have occasionally rescued the human spirit from the darkness of historical circumstance, the movies appeared when Western civilization began to suffer its most profound crisis—the decay of language as the principal support of all human values. Almost as miraculous is the fact that the movies continue to grow. The growth of the movies as an ever-fresh narrative possibility remains a moral and esthetic alternative to the intellectual malaise that lingers painfully even after the collapse of the word in its traditional role as the perpetuator of ethical precepts and esthetic principles. But perhaps as noteworthy is the fact that the movies have never threatened to replace the word; much less have they claimed to displace it. The continued growth of the movies more than half a century after the birth of the talkies attests to their capacity to work with rather than against verbal narration.

Within such a historical context, *Seven Beauties* readily distinguishes itself by the completeness and sophistication with which it illustrates the creative dilemma of contemporary cinematic narration.[1] On the one hand *Seven Beauties* discloses a capacity to rescue the protagonist, Pasqualino, from his spiritual aimlessness by enacting a visual relation through which he is empowered to grow creatively. On the other hand, the movie exhibits a marked reluctance to explore the new values made possible through visual narration, that is, through visual relations capable of morally and esthetically extending the life of the protagonist.[2] Paradoxically, then, there is in *Seven Beauties* no pretense that a creative freedom can be achieved through means other than those offered by the living image, however tenuous a "thing" the living image is in the story. Conversely, it is clear that the verbal narration in *Seven Beauties* never tries to delude itself (or its audience) that words can once again be the exclusive or preeminent source of moral and esthetic liberation (witness the death of the three intellectuals—Francesco, the Anarchist, the Socialist—all men of words, all men with a message).[3] Hence the basic narrative dilemma of *Seven Beauties*.

The fundamental method of inquiry in this chapter is patterned after two contrasting sequences that clearly express the narrative ambivalence of *Seven Beauties*. The first of these is the courtroom sequence. The second is the final sequence of the movie, Pasqualino's return to postwar Naples. The former holds the promise of Pasqualino's salvation through the innocent image of a girl and through his own fleeting vision of her as a regenerative force.[4] The latter discloses nothing but the degeneration of those possibilities, perhaps in the image of the girl herself, but certainly in terms of Pasqualino's abuse of her image by virtue of his articulation of the ultimate aims of his life in relation to what he sees, if he does indeed see anything. Shortly after the verdict is announced in the courtoom sequence there is a cut from the shot of the despondent Pasqualino to an extreme close-up of the girl's face. She smiles lovingly and then wipes a tear from her eye. Another cut to Pasqualino shows his eyes returning to their blank stare, as if incredulous that among the welter of static and oppressive images in the courtroom there could be one that can so capture his eye. But almost immediately his eyes shift to the girl again, confirming beyond all doubt that there is indeed a redeeming image, and simultaneously singling out the life of that specific image as the source of his salvation.

In a flash, between the cut from Pasqualino to the girl, a new, living relation is born. In the second cut the creative power of that relation is confirmed. In other words, initially the visual lure renews the life of the eye, making it move. Eventually, the captivating image renews Pasqualino's flagging life and miraculously generates in him an esthetic longing that is clearly born of his heretofore untapped visual resources. It is thus in the courtroom sequence that the promise of Pasqualino's spiritual and imaginative regeneration is immediately evident. And such a promise is present only in the form of the vital visual relationship between Pasqualino and the girl, especially as the relationship intensifies, toward the end of the sequence.

And the triumph of the spiritual union issuing from the visual act between Pasqualino and the girl is all the more glorious because it entails a victory over Pasqualino's earlier revulsion at seeing that his seven sisters have become whores. Yet more: it is the potential fulfillment of the powers of cinematic narration that is born of the spontaneous, unmediated union of the seeing and the seen. The birth of cinematic narrative is no whimsical ploy to get the story going. It is capable of leading the two participants in it into energized relations that promise to liberate them so that they may get on with the supremely moral task of *increasing* life. The union of the seeing and the seen is the new way in which Pasqualino's earlier advice to the girl (that she "worry about growing up") becomes a positive freedom, a freedom to develop the visual and imaginative possibilities that dwell in the vital relation between eye and image. The growth of the girl's hair, now beyond shoulder length, is an indication of her growth as an image—of her growth as the union of the physical and the spiritual.

But growth is not an event belonging to the girl alone. Pasqualino also grows. He is now a participant in a relation whose liberating possibilities he had previously been unaware of. He is born into a world of cinematic values. But his birth is not only important because of what his relation with the girl is, but because of what it can be, even beyond the enlightening visual relation. There is now no other world for the two individuals but the one they have created from their own visual and imaginative centers. Even as the carabinieri remove Pasqualino from the courtroom, his eyes remain adoringly on the girl's image, hers on his.

The new narrative energies accordingly reveal an esthetic of action, that is, an esthetic in which the object of visual delight quickens a passion for the further enhancement of its own life. And the selfsame narrative energies reveal a morality of creativity as well as a new truth, a truth which, unencumbered by logic and dead symbols, expresses a fineness of distinction that attains to the immanent divinity within the reach of a "new man"—beyond the Anarchist's fondest dreams—whose active eye is the source of his newness.

Such is the basic importance of the courtroom sequence. In the last sequence, however, the humanistic consequences of the birth of cinematic narration die. Indeed the last sequence, entailing above all else Pasqualino's abuse of the girl's image, is the result of the steady attenuation of the creative possibilities announced in the courtroom. Disdainful of the living image before him, Pasqualino in the end "sees" vicious abstractions, sees "the ones" "out there." The postwar Naples to which he has returned—the postwar Naples which does not require that he live as a mere vestige of his prewar narrative impulses—allows Pasqualino to extend the potentialities inherent in the girl's image as he sees it in the courtroom. Inasmuch as he wretchedly fails to perform such an imaginative feat, Pasqualino commits narrative suicide.

Central though they are in revealing the narrative dilemma of *Seven Beauties*, the two sequences to be examined in detail must be related to others in the story. The events of Pasqualino's life before the courtroom sequence are mainly characterized by his tribal ethic, by his conviction that his socially inherited notions of "honor" and "respect" are the essential elements of his life. His penchant for self-identity and his insistence on the purity of the family name are attributes of Pasqualino's hankering after honor and respect. In the courtroom Pasqualino loses that hankering. The courtroom sequence is accordingly the central event.[5] It divides the old Pasqualino from the new and announces a possible narrative alternative for him as a new man.

The final sequence must be considered in terms of events which are, on the whole, those after the courtroom sequence, beginning with the brief scene with the Socialist that marks Pasqualino's exile from Naples. After the courtroom sequence, when Pasqualino's socially inherited tribal ethic perishes, his motive force is generally characterized by his raw survival instinct.

But a merely chronological account of Pasqualino's narrative life in terms of "before" and "after" the courtroom sequence would be naïve. Surely *Seven Beauties* uncompromisingly demands that the opening black-and-white montage and voice-over narration be thoroughly accounted for in the total narrative scheme. Pasqualino's life is inextricably linked to that voice-over narration as well as to his own emergence onscreen, at the end of that montage, as the solitary color image out of the multitude of black-and-white ones, anonymous as well as historically identifiable, that precede it. At this point there is obviously insufficient evidence to determine the extent to which the verbal energies of the unseen voice-over narrator of the opening montage clarify the principal narrative thrust. For now, it will be convenient to incorporate into the text the voice-over narration of the opening montage. Visually, it begins over the monochrome image of Hitler. It continues until the explosion that accompanies the opening of Pasqualino's eyes and extends well into the transformation of Pasqualino into a color image in the forest. It may be noted that the litany about "the ones" readily discloses the narrator's attempt to classify all human acts cynically, that is, to deny human actions their uniqueness and to affirm nothing but their inherent destructiveness. It goes as follows:

The ones who don't enjoy themselves even when they laugh, Oh, yeah.
The ones who worship the corporate image not knowing that they work for someone else, Oh, yeah.
The ones who should have been shot in the cradle, Oh, yeah.
The ones who say, "Follow me to success but kill me if I fail, so to speak."
The ones who are noble Romans.
The ones who say, "That's for me."
The ones who voted for the right because they'd abolish strikes.
The ones who voted twice so as not to get dirty.
The ones who never get involved with politics, Oh, yeah.
The ones who say, "Try to be calm, try to be calm."
The ones who still support the king.
The ones who sing, "Oh, yeah."
The ones who make love standing in their boots and imagine they are in a luxurious bed.
The ones who believe Christ is Santa Claus as a young man, Oh, yeah.
The ones who say, "Oh, what the hell."
The ones who were there.
The ones who believe in everything, even in God.
The ones who listen to the national anthem.
The ones who love their country.
The ones who keep going, keep going just to see how it will all end, Oh, yeah.
The ones who are afraid of flying.
The ones who never had a fatal accident.

The ones who have had one.
The ones who at a certain point in their lives created the secret weapon,
   Christ, Oh, yeah.
The ones who always stand in the bar.
The ones who are always in Switzerland.
The ones who started early, haven't arrived, and don't know they're not
   going to, Oh, yeah.
The ones who lose wars by the skin of their teeth, Oh, yeah.
The ones who say, "Everything's wrong here."
The ones who say, "It's time for a good laugh," Oh, yeah, Oh, yeah,
   Oh, yeah.

The montage is part of the overall method of narration, finding its
counterpart within the action in color in the verbally initiated
"flashbacks," especially in the first one, when Pasqualino says to
Francesco, "I killed for a woman," and the camera tilts up the forest
trees and cuts to Concetti's patriotic thigh. The voice-over narration
and the flashbacks (which are really always revelations and thus
"flashforwards") contribute to the creation of an intricate and immanent structure that defies simplification. Within such an intricate
structure the end of the movie may well be its beginning, its beginning, in a very special way, the expression of its finality. After all,
Seven Beauties begins and ends with freeze-frames.
   The two sequences to be described in detail will serve as general
models from which the narrative and humanistic significance
enacted in the movie through Pasqualino's agency can be accurately
elicited. For instance, the extent to which Pasqualino is free (or
"alive") at the end of the story can be determined in relation to the
contrasting creative possibilities that he can envision in the girl's
image toward the end of the courtroom sequence and in the final
one. The degree to which Pasqualino is in the end "ready" (as is the
girl) to extend the actuality of growth that is visually established in
the courtroom is a second example of the significance of these two
sequences. And the relation between Pasqualino's affirmation of his
existence (at the end) and his future capacities as narrator, if any,
can be seen in direct relation to an examination of *Seven Beauties*
focused on these two contrasting sequences.
   Now the girl, of course, is present earlier in the story. In that
earlier scene, in fact, Pasqualino himself articulates the promise of
growth. He consoles the girl, who cries because she can't sing well,

saying to her, "If anyone bothers you, say you're my fiancée. Just tell him: 'I'm engaged to Pasqualino Seven Beauties.'" The girl, now smiling, says, "But it's not true," and Pasqualino replies, "Not now. But later, who knows? Just worry about growing up. Now sing me a song." The girl goes off grinding the organ, singing a song in celebration of life for its own sake; she is visibly happy.[6] Pasqualino goes off in the opposite direction, his face showing clear pride, if not outright vanity, at having been able to melt away the girl's troubles.

But while the relationship of this scene to the courtroom sequence cannot be ignored, it must be noted that all the other events in the sequence in which the scene appears deny to the first encounter the import of the relation between the girl and Pasqualino in the second, at the courtroom. First, Pasqualino's words of consolation to the girl disclose his reliance on his self-concept, that is, on his identity as a man women "go for" (as he later expresses it to Francesco in the concentration camp). In other words, Pasqualino sees himself in a position of superiority over the girl by virtue of his notoriety as a lover.

Furthermore, Pasqualino's words of consolation are like a verbal talisman whose power comes from the respect that he presumably commands in Naples. (Shortly before the beginning of this sequence, Pasqualino puts an automatic pistol under his belt and says to his mother, "This pistol keeps me out of trouble. It means respect.")

Also, it is obvious that at this earlier time, the girl is for Pasqualino merely one of many women in whom he shows interest. Immediately after he leaves the girl, a plump, more mature-looking woman playfully tells Pasqualino to leave the girl alone, and Pasqualino just as playfully tells her, "Jealousy's not nice." As he continues to walk down the street, another young woman blows kisses at him from a balcony. Still another, the young seamstress behind the sewing machine on the side of the street, smiles coquettishly at him. And halfway down the massive steps leading to the Galleria a long shot shows him stopping briefly at the steps and giving one of the two young women there the flower from his lapel.

Finally—and what is most important to the distinction between the first and the second encounter with the girl—Pasqualino is on his way to meet Don Raffaele for the first time. Don Raffaele's ascendancy over Pasqualino entails above all else the requirement that both Pasqualino and his family be honored and respected. Don Raffaele's own dominance over Pasqualino (and thus the immediate suggestion of a hierarchy of honored and respected men) is affirmed in the visual relation between the two men. Don Raffaele talks to Pasqualino from the high shoeshine chair with the small eagle figure on the top of the chair's back. As in the opening shots of Hitler and Mussolini addressing the anonymous masses, Don Raffaele, the local "fascist" power, dictates to Pasqualino from on high, telling him that he must take certain actions because of others that he has failed to take. Don Raffaele says that Pasqualino has failed to gain respect and honor for his family, and tells him, almost commands him, to "go see" for himself at the Palonetto (the brothel) the social disgrace of Concetti, who "has shoes with red bows" (meaning that she is a prostitute). Thus Don Raffaele further involves Pasqualino in the abstractions of honor, respect, and the family in which Pasqualino is already sufficiently involved, as is evident in his earlier words to Concetti in front of the dressing room mirror, at the vaudeville theater: "We haven't got a penny. I'm a man with seven sisters. I've got to defend our honor! It's all we've got."

What Don Raffaele tells Pasqualino to "see" at the Palonetto is the image of Concetti, the image of a woman who lives on the *verbal promise* of marriage that Totonno has presumably made to her. Concetti is the woman whose ethical disaster is the result of belief in words. For this reason her prostitution, unlike the girl's, much later in the story, never goes beyond the merely pathetic. There is never an indication that Concetti's life could have been creatively changed through a relationship with Totonno. (Consider the fact that not once in *Seven Beauties* are Totonno and Concetti seen together in one shot; and for that matter, consider the fact that there is not a shred of empirical evidence that they ever directly see each other.) Concetti's "love" for Totonno is therefore tainted by an abstraction of a twofold character: she is the victim of an empty verbal promise and, as a result, she fails to enact a creative union with the man who *tells* her he will marry her.

And certainly nothing could be further from Don Raffaele's intentions than that Pasqualino should "see" for "himself," that is, that he should see as the individual that he so clearly is when he sees the angelic image of the girl in the courtroom. At this time Pasqualino's function is limited to confirming the moral judgment that Don Raf-

faele has passed on Concetti and, by extension, on Pasqualino himself; and what is more, Pasqualino is to make certain that Totonno's
transgression against the family's honor and respect does not go
unavenged. Just as certainly, what Pasqualino sees as a result of Don
Raffaele's command, that is, Concetti in the brothel, is a far cry from
what he sees by himself, acting out of his own center of visual
energy, toward and up to the end of the courtroom sequence. Pasqualino's credulous submission to Don Raffaele's demands only ac-
centuates the calamity of his own life.

The courtroom sequence is evidence that the reverence for the
institutional abstractions of the family and of honor and respect that
result in Pasqualino's imprisonment are no longer motive forces in
his life. That all these socially inherited abstractions have perished is
made clear by the disarmingly all-important fact that the spoken
word is absent throughout the sequence. (The only sound is the
music, a wind and string version of the song the girl sang in the
street. Thus the sequence announces the celebration of life that is
about to take place, especially between seer and seen. The only
words are those seen in the symbolic images of the mural and in
front of the magistrate's podium.) In such a wordless world, the way
is clear for the enactment of a new process of creating human relations between individuals, despite the fact that the courtroom is a
microcosm of the social forces that put Pasqualino's tribal ethics on
trial.

Pasqualino's role as the protector of his family also ends as soon as
the camera shows his physical separation from his sisters and his
mother in the courtroom. This severing of the familial bond is even
more pronounced when contrasted to that earlier scene, just before
he ventures out into the streets of Naples, when Pasqualino draws
the bedsheet curtains to separate himself and his family from the
rest of the relatives. Once in the world of the family unit, Pasqualino
warns his mother and sisters to beware of Uncle Nick and his family,
tells his mother to stop feeding the sisters bread and onions, and
gives her money to buy some eggs to "put some color" in the homely
sisters' pale cheeks. Thus here Pasqualino had singled himself out as
the center of family life, as its adviser, protector, and provider. In
the courtroom sequence, however, the role of family head belongs
altogether to the lawyer, who feeds on the prostitution of the sisters

and receives their congratulations and adoration after the court allows Pasqualino's insanity plea.

The death of Pasqualino's obsession with honor and respect, and thus the death of his essence as a "social" man, can be found in his visual relations to other images in the courtroom. Throughout the proceedings Pasqualino is in the defendant's box. In the long shots—such as those when the camera sees the magistrate come into the far end of the courtroom—the box is seen to be equidistant between the bench and the gallery, to the left of the former and to the right of the latter. The defendant's box, quite simply, is framed. But it is not framed only by legal officials and spectators, for these are themselves framed by symbolic images, representative of the "imperishable" abstract powers of which they are but the temporal custodians. Behind and above the bench is the equestrian statue, reminiscent of the one that frames Don Raffaele when Pasqualino goes to see him after murdering Totonno. There is accordingly a strong suggestion that Don Raffaele and the magistrate wield equal power over the individual, that the criminal and the legal forces differ only in the method in which they annihilate the life of the individual.[7] Behind and above the gallery is the baroque mural of symbolic legal images, the details of which form the opening shots of the sequence. The first of these details, a woman in flowing robes and armored breast cups holding a spear in her left hand and a shield in her right, announces that the world in which Pasqualino will soon appear must be defended from the likes of Pasqualino. The next detail is a woman who cradles a lawbook on her right arm and carries a standard with a Latin inscription expressing a prohibition in her left hand. This image proclaims that the instrument for defense is the law, and that the law is inherently negative. Two cherubs pointing their trumpets downward summon mere mortals to the lofty world of legal abstractions. The crown, another detail, is itself crowned by an orb. From the crown fall drapes that are held open by angels at each side. And beyond the drapes is still another crown with a scale of justice immediately beneath it. Between the two ends of the scale is a book, and framing the crown, in front of the scale and behind the book, are a sword (on the left) and a trident (on the right) whose points meet just below the book. The world of transcendental abstraction reveals more of its disdain for life in this world. The more depth it unfolds, the more it shows that it is itself supported by ethereal and static images before which Pasqualino's own image, which is the first living image after the shots of the mural, is totally powerless. And Pasqualino is also framed by the two carabinieri who stand guard at opposite ends of the defendant's box. He is, of course, captive within the box itself. From both ends of the courtroom the representations of legal power declare Pasqualino's insignificance as an individual, his mere presence there as an "ugly little worm," as Totonno calls him earlier. Thus, ironically, Pasqualino's demands for honor and respect—so freely made of Concetti at the vaudeville theater, of all the sisters in his own house, of the women in the streets of Naples, and of Totonno at the Palonetto—are lost in the trappings of a legal and symbolic system whose own demands for honor and respect disclose its contempt for the individual who seeks the same honor and respect.

In declaring Pasqualino's ethical commitments scurvy and despicable, however, the social structure also proclaims its own moral ineffectiveness. And this double irony acquires a further measure of significance because the entire courtroom sequence is silent. There are no words spoken as a dialectical refutation of Pasqualino's actions. There are only the dead symbols, the vapid pomp of the court, the prostituted sisters. Social morality is therefore dead, both in the individual and in the body politic.

In direct relation to his notions of honor and respect and the fate they suffer in the courtroom sequence, Pasqualino's first encounter with the lawyer, as well as his second meeting with Don Raffaele, ought to be considered relevant to the courtroom sequence. In the detention jail, when the lawyer tells him that the only alternative to a death sentence is an insanity plea, Pasqualino, insulted, responds, "Me? I'm a man of honor. I [committed the murder] as an act of honor. I won't be a clown!" Soon the enraged lawyer replies, "If you prefer your stupid honor, I won't help you and you're as good as dead. Make up your mind: your life or your honor." Pasqualino's very presence in the courtroom discloses his choice for life over his inhibitive concepts of honor and respect.

And as to his second meeting with Don Raffaele, Pasqualino's presence in the courtroom is more than sufficient evidence that he has willingly forfeited that "50 percent of the moral profit" ("respect") which Don Raffaele tells him is all that he can hope to reap after his "unimaginative" handling of Totonno's killing. According to Don Raffaele the other 50 percent of the moral profit is freedom. But Don Raffaele's notion of freedom never goes beyond the crude fascist notion of freedom as power over the weak masses. It is therefore of little consequence that in view of Don Raffaele's ethical precepts Pasqualino, once in the courtroom, is a moral bankrupt. In fact, it is a great benefit for Pasqualino that his socially inherited ethical assets are reduced to nothing. As is evident throughout the courtroom sequence, *morality* (in the active sense of that word, as *conduct*, as *creative behavior*) has nothing to do with dominating over or being feared by others. It has more to do with the eventual opening of Pasqualino's liberated eye, with seeing, and with imagining the welter of creative possibilities that issue from the encounter with the individual image.

The loss of identity announces the birth of individuality. Such is fundamentally the regenerative process enacted in the courtroom. The law's contempt for Pasqualino and its inability to offer an alternative morality at once cancel Pasqualino's identification with its impotent ideals of social order, justice, honor, and respect and declare nothing but the death of the bond between the individual and society. There can be no more narrative by abstract identification because there is nothing—no socially inherited concept of honor, no family, no ethical order—for Pasqualino to identify with.

Yet once stripped of the weight of social narration, Pasqualino becomes immediately receptive to the beneficent powers of the image—to its powers to create a new relation, a new narrative out of the dark void of his previous existence as a man with an identity. Society, of course, is not as fortunate. That it does not have at its disposal the new narrative means is borne out by the fact that the most creative event in Pasqualino's life takes place within the social sanctum at the very moment that the magistrate condemns Pasqualino to imprisonment. The life of the individual thus becomes the only creative power potentially allowing him to reap an abundance of new moral profits.

This is not to say that Pasqualino's readiness to live by the image is the result of an exclusively subjective "change of mind." His ego, that is, the intellectual sense of permanence that had earlier allowed him to reduce his life to an identity, is now dead. Pasqualino does not will himself into a new vision. Consider the fact that, as an extension of his penchant for identity and self-classification, seeing his sisters has been an evil. To see the sisters as whores, as he so obviously does in the courtroom, is to see them abstractly; it is to see a *class* of images that is morally unfit because an "intellect" so mediates between eye and image in favor of such a judgment.[8] So it is more accurately speaking the image, the enlightened "object" which hurls itself in the way of his vision to bring about Pasqualino's rebirth at the moment when, with downcast eyes, he passively surrenders his visual energies to the calamity that he "sees" in the images of his sisters. The dark shadow across Pasqualino's face in the early shots of the sequence is no trivial detail, for initially he sees the realm of the image through the dark shadow of his socially inherited ethical ways.

But now his eye—free from the burden of words, of the past, of ethics, of society—marries, joins the image of its salvation. In the immediate and in the unique, Pasqualino discovers the possibilities for a new life. Without willing it, he discovers, in the eye itself, his own image as the possible new image of man in all its divine splendor. Pasqualino discovers the source of his potential divinity in his own human vision as well as in the girl's human image.

If the courtroom sequence is a living model of what can be in terms of a new narrative possibility, the last sequence is the final, dead testimony of what could have been and was not. There are, however, two intervening sequences that foreshadow the narrative dilemma itself.

The first such sequence is Pasqualino's perverse sexual encounter with the sick woman at the insane asylum. The second is his even more perverse sexual intercourse with the female commandant of the concentration camp. These intervening sequences relate also to Pasqualino's residual freedom in the end. In the end Pasqualino's image is frozen on the screen. He is going nowhere, or at least he is not going anywhere as a new man. But in reality this last image of *Seven Beauties* is only a magnified moment that illustrates Pasqualino's failure to transform his freedom from the calamities of war into a creative freedom. The fact is that the intervening sexual encounters illustrate the process whereby Pasqualino narrates himself into captivity. As much as any other sequences after the courtroom sequence, the two sexual encounters and the relations they create show the regression of Pasqualino's humanity and the concomitant attenuation of his narrative powers.

Taking place almost immediately after the courtroom sequence (only the brief scene with the Socialist intervenes), Pasqualino's rape of the sick woman is the first indication that he is incapable of assimilating the creative powers of vision beyond the presentational instance of the courtroom sequence. To make love, if so it can now be called, for him entails dominance over the image; it involves the abuse of the image.

At first Pasqualino is visually attracted to the woman, who is bound hand and foot to her hospital bed. He lifts her hospital robe to look at her naked body. But here looking leads to nothing creative. It is not the enactment of a promise of growth, but the failure of the eye, now as sick as the image, to see that the immobile woman cannot be the bearer of creative energies such as are embodied in the girl. Nonetheless Pasqualino gags the woman, slaps her, calls her a "stupid, filthy whore," and rapes her.

The creative visual possibilities enacted in the courtroom are short-circuited by Pasqualino's incapacity to see differences of kind between individual images, and just such an incapacity summarily dismisses all creativity from his encounter with the sick woman. With its reference to the female image as "whore" and with its exclusive aim at the satisfaction of a barren passion, the rape scene is also a prelude to Pasqualino's eventual verbal abuse of the girl.

Moreover, since the image of the sick woman lacks the narrative energy of the girl's, the rape scene announces the narrative disaster at the end; it exhibits the natural inability of the image to requite an eye which no longer adores it but which instead violates it by "seeing" in it nothing but the reflection of its own perversity. This means that after the death of his socially inherited desire for honor and respect in the courtroom sequence, the general condition of Pasqualino's life is such that he becomes what he sees without ever imagining the possibilities for creativeness or destructiveness in what he sees.

Thus the net result of Pasqualino's perverse way of seeing the sick woman is that he ends up just like her. Immediately after the rape scene, two orderlies spray Pasqualino with a fire hose, then beat him senseless and put him in a straitjacket. Then, after the electroshock treatment, the camera sees him from above, strapped securely to the bed, a piece of cotton stuffed in his mouth. Seeing the woman in bonds results in his becoming a powerless, motionless, sick image himself. The image that he believes will free him of his sexual desires renders him an imaginative as well as a physical prisoner.

It is, after all, imagination that Pasqualino lacks more than anything else. He lacks a sustaining liberating power, having its source in his ability to see the possibilities of visual relations, which would allow him to discriminate between the creative and the inhibitive, the captivating and the captive. It is for this reason that the regenerative process in the courtroom is not actually initiated by Pasqualino. It is also for this reason that the creative possibilities of that process die with the courtroom sequence. He becomes what he sees. The image of the moment, angelic or satanic, pure or corrupt, transforms him at the same time that he is incapable of imagining values in such transformations.

Already before his encounter with the sick woman—or for that matter before he sees the girl in the courtroom—Pasqualino's imaginative ineptness is a dominant pattern in his life. For example, in the streets of Naples, seeing the young women who adore him makes Pasqualino a gentle and tolerant man of the world. But at the end of that sequence, when he confronts Totonno at the Palonetto, he becomes or tries to become, a man who can "command respect," such as Don Raffaele himself. Having just before seen the image of Don Raffaele, it is only natural for Pasqualino to try to narrate himself into a life such as the Don's. In neither of these two instances does Pasqualino create, imagine, his life as an individual. Instead, his life is intellectualized for him by ready-made social concepts. In relation to the young women, Pasqualino readily adopts the concept of the worldly lover. In relation to Totonno, he adopts the concept of a man who commands respect. But in both cases his actions are, at least implicitly, imposed upon him by sheer weight of social convention. Thus the power that social convention has over Pasqualino inhibits whatever powers for individual growth he may at this time possess. The courtroom sequence shows that, Don Raffaele's definition of it notwithstanding, imagination is the vision of possibilities for moral and esthetic growth in the individual image. Furthermore, the courtroom sequence shows that imaginative vision belongs to the individual only as a direct result of his freedom from the dumb, habitual practice of social ethics. The imagination is thus the only active moral power. Its actions are and can only be—as in the courtroom—visions of immanent value.

The structure of the action after the courtroom sequence supplies clearer evidence of Pasqualino's unimaginative relations to what he sees. In the courtyard of the Naples prison Pasqualino refuses to do calisthenics and instead begins to deliver a speech in imitation of Mussolini. The other prisoners, on the other side of the fence, mockingly chant, "Duce! Duce!" as the prison guards drag Pasqualino away. And later, in the detention station where Pasqualino and the Socialist await transportation, Pasqualino looks up at the photograph of Mussolini that hangs above them. Shortly after, Pasqualino says to the Socialist, "I kind of like Il Duce, you know. He built roads, gave us an empire, made the other countries respect us. When he speaks—that voice, those eyes! . . . Now they all envy us. They used to spit at us Italians, remember? Then all those strikes and riots. The country was a mess. He put everything in order." Eventually, toward the end of this chapter, it will be possible to affirm that the relation between Pasqualino and Mussolini is no narrative whim, that Pasqualino becomes a "fascist" narrator.

But a central and even more direct illustration of Pasqualino's failure as imaginative man can be found in the contrast between the references to the imagination made by Pasqualino after he gets rid of Totonno's body and by the psychiatrist shortly after Pasqualino rapes the sick woman.

After he dispatches Totonno's remains to Genoa, Milan, and Palermo, Pasqualino says to Don Raffaele over the telephone, "Just like you said, imagination." Pasqualino's "imagination" turns him into a butcher. It also results in his arrest. Moreover, Pasqualino is incapable of "imagining" that Concetti's love for Totonno, even if it is based on a mere verbal promise, is stronger than her own sense of honor and respect or than her loyalty to the family. But more important, he is incapable of imagining that the imagination has little to do with social concepts of honor and respect, and absolutely nothing to do with the destruction of a life for the sake of honor and respect. And just after the courtroom sequence, Pasqualino tells the Socialist that he will befriend a doctor or a nurse at the insane asylum. He will "get organized," he says. The scene ends with Pasqualino's pathetic repetition of Don Raffaele's earlier words: "Naples is the land of imagination."

Not surprisingly, after the rape of the sick woman, when the psychiatrist warns Pasqualino that the war "may be worse than anything [he] can imagine," Pasqualino responds: "Nothing could be worse than here. I'll do anything to get out. I'll do anything to live!" A cut away from the flashback scene of the insane asylum shows Pasqualino standing in the middle of the concentration camp courtyard. His hands clasped behind his neck and his eyes half-shut with exhaustion suggest—if the previous concentration camp sequences have not already done so—that the insane asylum was a paradise by comparison. But Pasqualino is unable to imagine the worst, just as in the end he is unable to imagine the best.

During his second meeting with Don Raffaele, before Don Raffaele tells Pasqualino of all the ways to dispose of a body ("the king-size coffin," "the cement shoes," etc.) he says to him, "Normal people can't even imagine, understand?" Before the psychiatrist warns Pasqualino against the horrors of war, she says to him, "You've done terrible things, but you're normal." The *norm* of Pasqualino's life is unimaginativeness.

Without imagination he therefore acts on mere survival instinct. This instinct that drives him to the very end of the story is best articulated in the anecdote the commandant tells him after he finally manages to "make love" to her: "In Paris," she says, "a Greek made love to a goose. He did this to eat, to live. And you, subhuman Italian larva, you found the strength for an erection. That's why you'll survive and win in the end. You subhuman worms with no ideals or ideas. And our dreams for a master race—unattainable."9 Indeed, Pasqualino's life after the courtroom sequence is in many ways the monotonous expression of a survival urge altogether unqualified by creative direction. For this reason Pasqualino's procreative impulse, especially as expressed to Francesco immediately after the slaughter of the prisoners in the courtyard, bears no genuine creative passion. Pasqualino's "will" to have children and to see his children's children ad infinitum is nothing but a particular facet of his instinct to endure beyond the shock of seeing the slaughter of the prisoners. The Anarchist interrupts Pasqualino's raving, pronouncing the procreative urge so much "bullshit." And, much to

Pasqualino's distress (and, it might be added, incomprehension),
the Anarchist continues:

The more children you have, the faster the end will come. In 1400 there
were 500 million people on the earth. By 1850 there were twice that, one
billion. We get indignant over 20 or 30 million dead. But in three hundred
years there will be 30 billion of us. The whole world will be as crowded as
we are here. People will kill for a slice of bread. Whole families will be
slaughtered for an apple. And the world will end. Too bad, because I
believe in man. But in a new man that must be born: a civilized man. Not
that "intelligent" man who has tilted nature's balance and destroyed
everything—a new man who can rediscover harmony within himself.

The beliefs of the Anarchist run counter to Pasqualino's impulses.
But what is more, within the larger context of the story they are vital
in pointing out the barrenness of Pasqualino's procreative dreams,
especially when, at the end, Pasqualino adopts his own warped version of the Anarchist's Malthusian prediction to justify his own urge
for survival. When the girl reappears at the end, she is the innocent
victim of Pasqualino's aimless procreative urge.
    The procreative urge—with its emphasis on the mere quantita-
tive increase of life—is from the beginning aimed only at self-
preservation. The only creature capable of transforming the
monotonously quantitative into the actually qualitative is the girl.
The girl is the only image in which Pasqualino's procreative urge
becomes a creative craving, becomes the object of a yearning to
grow in a world of new values. But the girl is displaced by the sick
woman, who is in turn replaced by the commandant. That a creative
ideal ceases to be a concern of Pasqualino is further borne out by the
relation established between the commandant and Pasqualino's
mother, and by the later relation between Fifi, Pasqualino's "first
love," and the food he eats so as to manage an erection and seduce
the commandant.
    Soon after the massacre to the accompaniment of the waltz, the
camera, acting as an extension of Pasqualino's eye, moves closely on
the commandant's face. It then cuts away to the image of a young
boy, then back to the face of the commandant. Subsequently, there
is a montage consisting of quick cuts from the commandant's face to
Pasqualino's mother's face. In the short scene that follows, the
mother teaches a lesson to the boy: "Women are women. Even the

wickedest of all. If you can go to her heart, like the song says: 'Brigida with your ways, you are like a cup of coffee: bitter on top but sweet at the bottom. And so I have to stir you to bring the sugar to my lips.'"

The connection between the slaughter of the prisoners and the commandant's face and the connection between the child's image and the mother's face are visual and moral poles apart. The image of the woman in the world Pasqualino now inhabits is the immediate cause of the destruction he witnesses. The relation of the commandant to the slaughter scene is no doubt a lesson in its own way—an object lesson in evil, in fact. It is accordingly the opposite of the mother's, which is a lesson on the discovery of the good. But the mother's lesson, a product of Pasqualino's memory, is clearly obsolete if only by virtue of that earlier connection between the commandant and the slaughter of the men. And yet the relation, the narrative that Pasqualino intends to generate with the repulsive and destructive image of the commandant is altogether based on the mother's lesson, given to him in a past that is totally unrelated to his present condition.

Nevertheless, as is made abundantly clear when he paraphrases it to Francesco and later to the commandant herself, Pasqualino thoroughly believes in the applicability of his mother's lesson. Thus the condition that best describes Pasqualino's life just before his first attempt to seduce the commandant is, paradoxically, that he is about to become what he sees (the fascist image) while remaining blind to change as a fact of life. In fact, his blindness to change is evident in his implicit belief that "women are women." Pasqualino once more reasserts his predisposition to classify images, and thus again makes it clear that only during the courtroom sequence, through the agency of the angelic image, is he genuinely capable of seeing differences and of indicating his capacity to envision the good in those differences. The frail recollection of a useless lesson, finding the source of its applicability in the image that horrifies Pasqualino's eye, is a manifest indication that the survival impulse is totally unimaginative.

In other words, the difference between raw survival and creative craving is that, so far as the encounter with the commandant goes, Pasqualino's capacity to love can be measured only by the survival benefits which he believes mere sexual intercourse can guarantee.

This travesty of love is actually sheer animal desire. It is precisely on these terms that Pasqualino manages an erection once the commandant feeds him. As Pasqualino devours the food placed on the swastika-emblazoned rug, he tries to become sexually ready for his encounter with the commandant by remembering Fifi, his "first love." Immediately the connection is clear: the remembered image, like the food, nourishes, prepares, the body, but no more.

And what is immeasurably more important is that Pasqualino's use of the memory of his first love for sexual inspiration, like his use of the memory of his mother's lesson for guidance, enmeshes him more deeply in his uniquely calamitous relation with the commandant. The image of Fifi, appearing in a sort of vaudevillean version of *The Birth of Venus*, goes through three different stages in relation to the boy who sees her. Sometimes a child cries in fear, sometimes eyes appearing to belong to an older boy stare in delight, all while Fifi performs her seductive dance. And between the shots of Fifi and the boys' faces there are brief shots of a mature Pasqualino engaged in sexual intercourse with different women. Not once, however, are any of the participants in the sexual acts naked. As it was with the sick woman in the insane asylum, sexual intercourse is purely a matter of the gratification of an immediate desire; it is thus something hurried, furtive, and, most of all, something without creative consequences. The scenes that Pasqualino recalls for his sexual inspiration show him growing from a terrified child to an adolescent voyeur to a sexually mature man for whom physical intercourse is the "first," and ultimately the only, form of love. The girl is altogether absent from Pasqualino's remembrances. The fact is of little importance in the sequence. After all, only a foolhardy romantic would expect that in the face of so much disaster Pasqualino should pine for the girl like some latter-day Don Quixote for his Dulcinea. But at the end of the story, when the survival instinct is no longer a necessity in Pasqualino's life, the girl is on the verge of becoming no more than another Fifi.

Verbal expressions of Pasqualino's survival instinct abound, even in addition to those already cited. Early in the story, after witnessing the slaughter of the Jews, Pasqualino tells Francesco that "it would have been suicide" to try to stop the massacre. "My life has been disgusting," he says to Francesco later at the concentration camp, "but I like being alive." After he settles on the seduction of

the commandant as his way out of the concentration camp, he tells
Francesco that he won't give up the idea, justifying his plan by
saying, "I want to live." He knows that he wants to live but ignores
what he wants to live for. There are also numerous visual expressions of Pasqualino's barren survival instinct. In contrast to the verbal examples, however,
these are not affirmations of a primal will to endure; they are instead
indications that Pasqualino's sense of motion, coinciding with his
sense of freedom, is thoroughly negative. That is to say, his motions
are consistently *away from* rather than *toward* an action. Perhaps
the most obvious example of Pasqualino's peculiar form of motion is
his desertion from the Italian army. But his desertion turns out to be
only the first of a series of instances where motion is negative.
Shortly after his desertion there is his frantic dash away from the
scene of the slaughter of the Jews. He also runs away from the police
shortly after disposing of Totonno's body.

Pasqualino is not to blame for running from these threatening
forces. The war, the German soldiers, and the police threaten his
freedom. Also, it would be ridiculous to expect Pasqualino to take an
ethical stand such as the one Francesco suggests after the slaughter
of the Jews. Francesco's ethics are as negative as Pasqualino's sense
of survival. The question, however, remains: What does Pasqualino
run toward as he runs away? His desertion, as well as his flight from
the scene of the massacre, results in his capture by the Germans.
His attempt to escape the police (by far the best display of his
powers to move) ends when he stops on the balcony and shouts
across the rooftop at the policemen, "Give up, you'll never take
Pasqualino Seven Beauties alive!" He stops in order to proclaim
himself a man perfectly capable of retaining his freedom, his "moral
profit." As he shouts, the police enter the apartment, capture him
from behind, and it is Pasqualino who gives up, saying, "So I was
wrong."

Thus in the process whereby survival by running away becomes
the measure of Pasqualino's sense of freedom, flight also becomes a
senseless, mechanical habit. What makes Pasqualino run from the
forest villa? Here he finds a world of art (music, paintings, elaborate
ceiling and wall details). Nature and art are in harmony. Pasqualino
also sees an image of a woman whose man, to judge by his photograph on the piano, is either dead or off to war but certainly not

present. So Pasqualino also stumbles into a world that poses no threat to his freedom. The German granny doesn't speak a word while Pasqualino pillages the kitchen. Even a seemingly trivial detail—namely, that the smell of onions leads Pasqualino to the villa—becomes a part of the wholeness of his world at that moment. The smell of onions recalls his past in Naples, when he told his mother to stop feeding bread and onions to the sisters. Coupled with his reference to the granny as "mother," even his attraction to onions contributes to the suggestion that Pasqualino has found the safety of a home. Yet all he does is run away from the forest villa with his mouth and arms full of food, only, of course, to be captured by the Germans before he can even finish eating. Not once is there an indication that he wants to explore that world; not once is there even a hint that he can see the villa as a haven from his "disgusting" life.

The habit of running away remains with him to the very end, even when running away ceases to be a physical activity and becomes more properly a narrative deed. It is one of the supreme ironies of Pasqualino's life that the only moment he tries to move *toward* something is in the courtroom, where the carabinieri have to pull him away as he tries ever so futilely to get closer to the image of his redemption.

Both during and after Pasqualino's sexual encounter with the commandant his narrative dilemma, and by extension the movie's, becomes more difficult for three fundamental reasons. The first, already mentioned above, is that Pasqualino's survival, and not just the immediate gratification of his sick passion, is at stake in his attempted seduction of the commandant. The second is that the immediate visual connection that Pasqualino makes with the commandant bears not even the slightest trace of visual attraction. The third is the converse of the second, that is, that Pasqualino's eventual relation with the commandant makes him a captive both of his own survival urge and of the abstractions (the "ideals" and "ideas" of "a master race") by which the commandant lives. Of course Pasqualino does not become an ideological Nazi. He is an unwitting captive of the commandant's perversity; but then in all his unimaginativeness Pasqualino is always or almost always an unwitting captive of the event that happens to be narrating him at the time.

By the end of his encounter with the commandant, Pasqualino is
a fascist narrator. Needless to say, the term *fascist narrator* here has
none of the conventional ideological implications of fascism as a
political doctrine. It simply means one who narrates through the
abstract claim of superiority over other images for purposes that
ultimately inhibit the creative possibilities of both the dominant and
the dominated image. It is to be borne in mind that fascist narration
is really only a phase in Pasqualino's development (if such it can be
called), toward his more complex yet paradoxically more inhibited
condition as a man trapped by both his narrative capacities and his
narrative commitments. The more complex Pasqualino's life gets,
the more repressive it becomes. His survival instinct and his cynical
verbal narration (beginning with "Yes, I'm alive") are as essential to
his final condition as narrator as is his fascist narrative impulse.
Unlike the phenomenon of Life, which attains to creativity with
each step toward complexity, Pasqualino's life cannot affirm the
creative possibilities inherent in complexity, for his is in the end not
a life aiming at complexity but rather one merely resulting in moral
and imaginative confusion.[10]

The process whereby Pasqualino becomes a fascist narrator is
best illustrated by recourse to a specific narrative model, generated
by images, which begins during the sequence at the commandant's
office and extends to the visual relation of Pasqualino to the other
prisoners immediately after Francesco's execution and just before
the cut away to the final sequence. This model illuminates the range
of narrative implications of Pasqualino's attempt to seduce the
commandant and reveals the direct relation between his encounter
with the commandant and the final sequence.

During his first and unsuccessful attempt to make love to the
commandant, Pasqualino crawls up to her from the rug. The commandant awaits without emotion on the couch. Pasqualino kisses
her hand, then kisses his way up her arm, and finally smacks his
mouth on her right breast. He fails to arouse her sexually. The
camera cuts away to the commandant's face as she yawns. But suddenly her face takes on a serious expression, her eyes become alert
and shift upward and away to her right. A cut to Pasqualino's face
shows him looking at the commandant's eyes and then shifting his
eyes to what she is looking at. There is another cut. The black-and-

white photograph of Hitler's head that hangs on the wall behind the commandant's desk shows a vacant gaze; its eyes are focused on nothing; they look at an ideological world. After looking at the image of Hitler's head, Pasqualino gives up trying to arouse the commandant, saying, "I can't do it."

The commandant has in effect matched Pasqualino's masculinity against that of Hitler's abstract, disembodied image, and Pasqualino has come out the loser. In addition, Hitler's masculinity, itself clearly an abstraction, manifests itself to the commandant in terms of the "ideals" and "ideas" that are the measure of her life, of those "dreams of a master race" threatened by Pasqualino's "Mediterranean" racial "inferiority."

But more important in this brief scene is the fact that Pasqualino once again becomes what he sees. Looking into the commandant's face and seeing her eyes, he becomes the image of her eyes; and her eyes lead him to see Hitler's image. Once the source of direct contact with the angelic image, Pasqualino's eye is now an image that not only looks up to abstractions for its nourishment (that is, to the ideology, to the black-and-white image, to the head) but perversely adores the satanic superiority of an image that is even more lifeless than the images of the courtroom mural. The image of the commandant's eye forces Pasqualino to surrender his own eye to abstraction in an even more abject way than he did when confronted by the images of his sisters in the courtroom gallery.

Pasqualino's visual surrender, however, is only the immediate result of his encounter with Hitler's image. That in the end he is to a very definite extent the image of Hitler he sees in the commandant's office is made obvious in the movie's last shot. Like the photograph of Hitler, Pasqualino's last image looks at nothing. (Indeed, Pasqualino's vacant eye is seen earlier. During his second attempt to make love to the commandant, she says, "I want to see your eyes." She pries Pasqualino's eyelids open; there is nothing but an empty stare, an eye focused on nothing.) Pasqualino's final image, again like Hitler's, is that of a head without a body. And his is also a frozen, immobile image that, just before becoming static, has ever so ironically said, "Yes, I'm alive." Through his interaction with the image of abstraction and perversity Pasqualino becomes more than the rhetorical buffoon that he was when he imitated Mussolini at the detention prison.

Thus, again paradoxically, despite his failure to satisfy the commandant as a result of having been compared to Hitler's dead image, Pasqualino becomes what he sees, that is, a derivative of Hitler's image. His own living image becomes the mere imitation of the static black-and-white image of Hitler. It is accordingly as valid to say that the commandant judges Pasqualino to be inferior (a "worm") by virtue of his racial origin as it is to say that she judges his living-color image inferior by comparison to that dead, black-and-white one in which she locates her ideal of perfection. For Pasqualino to become what he sees eventually requires him to preside, as an agent for the "ideal" image (Hitler), over the indiscriminate destruction of other images (the prisoners) which are, by implication, "inferior" to the imitation (Pasqualino himself).

After the commandant feeds him, Pasqualino manages an erection. The commandant of course is as unmoved as if he hadn't succeeded. But she makes him the leader of his barrack and orders him to single out six men for extermination, saying, "It's your turn to play butcher." Once outside the commandant's office, in the barracks, Pasqualino is dressed in the dark blue coat and cap of the barracks leader. As he picks out the numbers of the prisoners at random, Francesco comes in and says, "No." Pasqualino replies, "Yes, it's our only way out." In his persistent ethical purity, Francesco warns: "We'll be like them." Pasqualino asserts his even more persistent survival instinct, saying, "We'll all die." "Then we'll all die," responds Francesco; and Pasqualino, now more than ever at a loss to justify his survival instinct, screams, "Go screw yourself! I'm the boss here!" Pasqualino is the loser in his dialectical bout with the ethical man. All he can do is assert his hierarchical superiority over Francesco.

But after the Anarchist's suicide, when Francesco breaks into his ethical frenzy, into his irrepressible affirmation of his humanitarianism by saying no to life, the commandant orders Pasqualino to execute Francesco. In a singular flash of ethical intuition Pasqualino says, "I won't shoot him." Yet just as the Anarchist makes it easier for Pasqualino to choose the six men to be exterminated by volunteering to die, Francesco helps him out of his first and only pure, intellectually motivated ethical crisis by asking Pasqualino to shoot him, as a favor, because life under the conditions of the concentration camp is worthless. Shortly after a shot of Pasqualino standing over the kneeling Francesco, there is a close-up of the cocked black Luger that a German officer puts in Pasqualino's hand. The gun aims point-blank at Francesco's head. It goes off. Francesco bleeds from the head; he falls forward, hunched over, dead.

It is clear enough that for Pasqualino, shooting Francesco means being "like them." Yet it is undeniable that firing the shot also means that Pasqualino partakes of Francesco's quintessential ethical character. Francesco's last moments as an ethical man enable Pasqualino to justify the execution as euthanasia, thus once again paradoxically allowing him to justify being "like them" through the beliefs of the character in the action who is least "like them." In short, Francesco's antifascist ethic directly results in confirming Pasqualino's birth as a fascist.

The shot Pasqualino fires extends beyond Francesco's death; it signals the end of all humanitarian ethics in their traditional form. And yet it also signals the birth of Pasqualino's warped ethical sense, that is, his beginning as a cynical narrator. As he is the imitation of the ideal fascist image, so is he the imperfect copy of the ethical ideal. The residual ethics of Pasqualino's negative expression ("I won't shoot him") find their initial transformation in his affirmation of his existence at the end of the movie ("Yes, I'm alive"). They find their most cynically refined form in the "Oh, yeah" refrain to the litany about "the ones" recited by the voice-over narrator during the opening montage. Moreover, the transition from the cynical affirmation of mere existence at the movie's end to the litany about "the ones" at the beginning is highlighted by the reappearance of the girl's song in the sound track at the very end. This time the voice is a man's, more than likely Pasqualino's own, which sings the once festive song in cynical mockery well after the disappearance of Pasqualino's dead, frozen image. In a word, Pasqualino's *yes* is the corrupt, cynical counterpart of Francesco's ethically pure yet equally life-denying *no*.

After a brief scene where German soldiers massacre more prisoners indiscriminately, the camera comes back to Pasqualino's hand. He still holds the cocked Luger, which now points down. The gun, the power that "would keep [him] out of trouble" reappears to immerse Pasqualino deeper in a self-centered world without narrative freedom. The camera then begins a slow ascent and a zoom-out. It shows Pasqualino standing, head bowed, in the foreground. The rest of the prisoners, faceless, anonymous, kneel submissively before him, forming endless rows that disappear in the mist in the deep background. Though the camera eventually abandons him as it continues to crane up and zoom out, Pasqualino stands above the images of the masses as Hitler's image hung above him at the commandant's office, as Mussolini's image hung above him at the detention station, as both Hitler's and Mussolini's images stood above the images of the masses during the opening montage. Within this context it is of more than passing interest to note that at different times the five fascists or dominant images of men in *Seven Beauties* look down at or stand above Pasqualino: Don Raffaele in his first meeting with Pasqualino; Hitler and Mussolini in the form of the black-and-white photographs that Pasqualino looks up at; Totonno after he knocks out Pasqualino at the Palonetto; and the lawyer when he leans over Pasqualino in the defendant's box. (The commandant also, as an extension of Hitler's master-race ideology, looks down from the balcony of her office at the distant image of Pasqualino, who stands alone in the center of the courtyard, his hands clasped behind his neck, while he sings a pathetic serenade at once intended to keep himself on his feet and to seduce the commandant. And as another extension of Nazi ideology, the two faceless German soldiers who capture Pasqualino and Francesco outside the forest villa appear as ominous figures standing over the two helpless Italians.) These visual relations suggest that Pasqualino can never become a "true fascist," that in relation to the dominant images he is always an image of mass man. Still, having shot Francesco, Pasqualino becomes, no matter how briefly, the "boss," the feared and dominant man, the "idol of the tribe" that he could not be in Naples.

But despite his becoming an imitation of both fascist and ethical man—or perhaps as a consequence of it—Pasqualino's narrative energies return him to his initial condition as mass man. For aside from Pasqualino there are only eight men in *Seven Beauties* whose images have visual individuality, but their "individuality" is linked not to their actions but to their beliefs.[11] Their individuality is accordingly burdened by a static identity which has been culturally, historically, socially, or intellectually acquired. Theirs is, in short, the aristocratic concept of individualism, not the democratic image of individuality. Now these men make up two clearly distinct classes. One of these groups consists of the five fascists or dominant images mentioned above: Hitler, Mussolini, Don Raffaele, the lawyer (as an extension of Don Raffaele's tribal powers but also as eventual pimp), and Totonno. The other group is made up of three antifascist idealists: Francesco, the Anarchist, and the Socialist. Pasqualino is the ninth man. He is a man without "dreams of a master race"; he is also a man without a belief in "a new man."

Thus since Pasqualino is never the bearer of a social or political ideology or of an ethical doctrine, and since he is also incapable of imagining his individuality as cinematic narrator, his relations to the other eight men come to indicate that Pasqualino's story is after all no more than the story of just one anonymous member of an indistinct group, mass man, upon whom social, political or humanitarian doctrines—in a word, archaic narrations—are imposed from outside. In other words, Pasqualino's story is one of his returning to his preindividualized form as an anonymous black-and-white image belonging to the faceless multitude of images in the opening montage. Ironically, then, his emergence on the screen as an individual opening his eyes and eventually moving in a unified world of color results in a movement, consistent with all of Pasqualino's other movements, *away from* a new, from a *cinematic*, individuality.

In the last sequence of the movie, the opening shots of a war-ravaged Naples soon give way to the bustling celebration of a new epoch. The old Naples that Pasqualino knew is dead. In this new postwar world, corresponding to the postverbal, cinematic world, Pasqualino cannot intellectually reenact the "real" verbal narrations of the idealogists. No doubt his eventual reliance on fascism, Malthusianism, and above all, cynicism, trap him in a narrative world that is no more. But just as clearly Pasqualino is totally incapable of reviving the humanitarian ardor of the idealists or the doctrinal fanaticism of the fascists. Accordingly, his narrative of survival in the final sequence is, to repeat, a confused instinctive atavism; it is not the product of intellectual conviction; it is an imitation of the "real" verbal narratives. Pasqualino cannot further his drive toward individuation through a commitment to such a mimetic narrative because this kind of narrative is no more than the mere result of his habitual survival instinct.

The stubborn fact confronting Pasqualino upon his return to Naples is that the world has changed. Either he changes with it or he perishes. Pasqualino's freedom therefore unequivocally resides in his capacity to grow as an image, to grow as cinematic man. The world of postwar Naples is after all the democratic world of images. The ubiquitous presence of American images in Naples (the soldiers, the sailors, the MPs, the cigarette packs, the dolls) illuminates beyond doubt the fact that the war as well as the verbally ordered world gives way to visual unity, to a new world, united by its transcendence of nationalities, where images are the central creative events.[12] No longer suppressed by the archetypal embodiments of archaic narrations, no longer suppressed by the need to survive, the images are free to grow and develop as so many individuals.

Yet in postwar Naples Pasqualino's disappearance as an image is already obvious. He is not visually present among the multitude of images that celebrate the new era. Instead his arrival is verbally announced by Concetti; and Pasqualino does not appear onscreen until he is in the family's house. (Indeed, the first image of Pasqualino in this the final sequence is a small black-and-white photograph of his face in an oval frame on a table in the house. The image is already on its way to becoming polarized, disembodied, static.)

Eventually the girl stands at the door. She sees the Pasqualino who has yet to appear as an image. The girl runs toward Pasqualino to fulfill the promise of the visual narrative enacted in the courtroom. And again, as in the courtroom, the visual narrative consists of a cross-cut of close-ups from the girl's face to Pasqualino's, which now appears for the first time in the sequence. Once more the girl's image brings Pasqualino to life, this time by rescuing him from his invisibility. But after his classification of the girl as "whore" and after his fascist-Malthusian lesson justifying procreation as a means to the unimaginative end of mere survival, Pasqualino turns away from the girl. His senseless habit of evasion is now tantamount to his suicide as an individual, to his disappearance as an image. Just as he turns away from the girl, his mother says, "Don't think about the past. What's done is done. Look at yourself, my son. You're beautiful. The war is over. Pasquali, you're alive." Still instructing Pasqualino in the creative life, the mother accurately locates the source of his freedom. She teaches him to forget about the verbally divisive and destructive world from which he has emerged. She also tells him to discover himself visually and to see in his own image that which is "beautiful," that which is alive, and that which can in turn see beauty.

But all Pasqualino "sees" is a divided image. His face is not reflected in the three-leaved mirror; because of his position it is lost between two divisions of the mirror, so that what is reflected is a faceless image. And since his back is almost altogether to the camera, it is as impossible to see the face of the image as it is to see its reflection. The image, in short, is not whole; so that even now it announces its eventual disappearance from the new world, implying the loss of Pasqualino's individuality and affirming his condition as mass man. Turning from the image (the girl) who has turned him into an image, Pasqualino in effect turns away from the source of his potential narrative freedom.

The camera then shifts angles and sees Pasqualino's face in the mirror. First it sees the divided face closer up. A shadow over the face indicates that Pasqualino's image has regressed to the darkness that afflicted it when it first appeared in the courtroom. But now that he has turned from the girl, has, that is, turned to himself, where there is no image and certainly no imagination, there is no hope for his narrative growth in the new world. When the black shadow disappears and Pasqualino's face appears in the mirror, he says, more to his cynical self than in response to his mother, "Yes, I'm alive." The words are powerless to affirm the life of the image because the image doesn't move, because, like the first images of Hitler and Mussolini, Pasqualino's last image is static, the captive of an obsolete and archaic narrative commitment that by verbally affirming the ego perversely denies the life of images as the new narrative energy.

And so, Pasqualino once more becomes what he sees. Rather, he becomes invisible because he doesn't see. In the train during the opening montage, even before the action turned from black-and-white to color, Pasqualino's individuality was announced by his eyes, which burst open in horror at an explosion which did not harm him but which instead announced his transformation into an image in living color. But in the final sequence the fate of the eye of the would-be individual is equal to the eventual fate of his image. Pasqualino doesn't see the girl. (Even in the cross-cuts to their faces Pasqualino already has the vacant gaze of Hitler's black-and-white

photograph, of his own last image.) Unable to see himself in a
condition where he is freely able to move toward the girl, he says to
her, "Even you have become a whore." Pasqualino's vision re-
gresses to those moments of his life, before his encounter with the
angelic image in the courtroom, and then afterward, at the insane
asylum, when he saw all women as whores.

The girl readily admits that she has become a whore, answering,
"Si." But at this point, where Pasqualino's narrative development
altogether hinges on how he sees one particular image, he remains
as blind to change as a condition of life as he was when he continued
to believe that "women are women." Once again incapable of seeing
differences, of seeing the transformations of a changing world, his
eye, a mere tool for classification, blinds itself to the possibilities for
narrative freedom visually discovered during the courtroom sequence.

But Pasqualino's visual energies are further vitiated by abstractions. His vacant eye, unexcited at the angelic image, directs the
girl's own eye toward what it itself cannot see, namely, the masses,
numbers, "the corporate image." "I want kids," he says to her, "lots,
twenty-five, thirty. We've got to defend ourselves. See all those
people? Soon we'll be killing each other for an apple. There's got to
be lots of us to defend ourselves, understand?" The camera never
follows Pasqualino's words, and thus "all those people" remain mere
words, visually less, in fact, than the multitude of anonymous images throughout the action. And so Pasqualino's vision of abstraction
commits him to becoming an abstraction himself. In the end his
narrative affinities lie with numbers, which is to say that, extended
to the voice-over narration of the opening montage, his narrative
affinities lie with "the ones." All he can "see" is numbers, which
means he can see nothing.

Within the context of such a narrative commitment on Pasqualino's part the girl is accordingly an unwitting whore. When she
replies to Pasqualino, "I've always loved you. I'm ready," she in
effect prostitutes her love to the timid, inhibitive narrative he envi-
sions for both of them as partners in that greater narrative venture,
life itself. The girl is now the victim of Pasqualino's blindness. And
Pasqualino's eye, once saved by the girl's image, now betrays her by
turning away from her and by leading her own eye to see and her

own image to be devoted to the most perverse "intellectual" abstractions. All growth in terms of visual narration has accordingly come to a dead end. That visual narration is no longer a creative alternative in Pasqualino's life is all the more obvious in the last shot of *Seven Beauties*. After Pasqualino says to himself, "Yes, I'm alive," he continues to stare into his own image. He never blinks. And this happens even before the camera, following Pasqualino's lead as a visually dead creature, signals its own blindness by freezing Pasqualino's already motionless image. Thus powerless to see value in the image that revived it in the courtroom, incapable of confirming the novelty of the individual image as a value, impotent as an imaginative force conducive to a vitally creative relation, and turned instead to itself as the instrument that annihilates its own narrative possibilities, Pasqualino's eye in its death truly marks him as a "monster," inhuman, as at once the murderer of the image and the victim of its corrupt way of seeing. He becomes what he sees, nothing, because nothing is what he sees. And equally, the paltry verbal affirmation of his existence comes to nothing because nothing vital, alive, cinematic, accompanies such an affirmation.

In the beginning of the story, then, Pasqualino's narrative powers are still in their degenerative process. Pasqualino's cynical affirmation of his existence and the concomitant disappearance of his image are found in the disembodied cynical narrator of the opening montage. Always a confused imitation of the original fascists or intellectuals, Pasqualino's voice-over narration indicates that he narrates in an ideological vacuum where the only possibility for verbal narration resides in the irony and the cynicism expressed by the mocking refrain, "Oh, yeah." All verbal affirmation is in fact a total denial.

With the death of ethics and ideologies as narrative forces, it is not surprising to find that the voice-over narrator denies even his own verbal capacity to give the story creative direction, including in the litany "The ones who sing, 'Oh, yeah.'" The one remaining verbal narrator never pretends that words can regain their narrative preeminence. And what is more, he has made himself part of "the ones." Pasqualino has returned to the masses. His only distinction as a member of the masses is his capacity narratively to speak about "the ones," to be more than ever blind to differences, to novelty, to individuality, to creativity. He is now the consummate classifier, not because he is an intellectual in the traditional sense, but because he is instinctively afraid to live in the boundlessly regenerative and creatively extensive world of an individual image, such as the girl's. Women are women, whores are whores, the ones are the ones, and the world is inherently evil.

Thus, like a Bergsonian hymenopteron, Pasqualino lives the life of instinct without intuitions, of order without unities, of strength without imaginative energies.[13] As the opening montage brings Pasqualino's story full circle, his eye will once more open, his image will again emerge miraculously into a world of color. He will be born as cinematic man, grow to see the angelic image as the source of his freedom, and die to the cinematic value of that image before he can enact a narrative that is the natural extension of his cinematic existence. He will then die, leaving nothing of value behind—except, of course, for the liberating genius of the narrative that might have been and was not.

Pasqualino's suicidal narration results in his total withdrawal into the invisible. Such a withdrawal from the only world in which growth and freedom are present is ultimately the consequence of both his obstinate refusal to change and his insistence on a permanent narrative base. In the end, because he can create only an egocentric world of hard-and-fast necessities, Pasqualino discovers nothing about his possibilities as a new narrative man. By mere instinct he locates or rather *re*locates his narrative base—the substance of his narrative wish—in his own past, in prewar Naples. In prewar Naples his narrative affinities fall squarely within the ready-made role of the dominant man—the role of preserving family integrity, and, by extension, of dominating over the larger communal life. And for all practical purposes Pasqualino's final narrative commitments likewise belong wholeheartedly to the perpetuation of totemism and tribalism.

If therefore there is a difference between the prewar and the postwar Pasqualino so far as his final condition as narrator goes, it is only because he has been able to cultivate and subsequently to express a vicious cynicism in relation to "the ones," which is to say in relation to all events. The difference is thus only one of degree that does not even approximate one of kind. Hence his voice-over narration at the beginning, which amounts to the culmination of his inexorable movement, if movement it can indeed be called, toward narrative by abstraction.

It is after all only through a persistent, albeit unmethodical, abstractive process that Pasqualino blunders into the fulfillment of his narrative wish for dominance over "the ones." Yet the significance of the consummation of Pasqualino's narrative wish is not nearly so crucial as is the obvious implication, inherent in his condition as invisible narrator, that the same abstractive process condemns him to a cyclical narrative with no genuine beginning, with no novelty, no birth. In the courtroom sequence the promise of narrative growth was the immediate result of the visual marriage between Pasqualino and the girl. The scene with the Socialist followed immediately, initiating the degenerative process whereby Pasqualino's potentialities for development as a new man began to atrophy.

The last sequence showed the net result of Pasqualino's development as a narrative monster, blind yet "looking" at abstractions, insensible to the image of rebirth embodied in the girl, destroyer of his own, the girl's, and the world's image. The opening montage is the confirmation of the fullest possible development of Pasqualino's monstrous narrative.

As both the final and the initial power in *Seven Beauties,* then, it is the invisible voice, not the living image, that supplies the narrative direction. It is not, however, as if the images die so the voice can be born. The voice is there from the start. And more than an indication of Pasqualino's passive withdrawal from a world of changing images, his voice is an active power that allows him to pass judgment on all life, even when the life about to unfold at the end of his voice-over narration is generated by his own actions as an image.

In his consistent drive toward an imperishable identity—which is the implicit motive force even in his survival urge—Pasqualino discovers such an identity in mere words. Invisible as he is in the beginning, then, he *is* the word, self-righteously omnipotent and omniscient, running his course as an image in the world of images only after his announcement of the primordial power of the word, and in the end rejecting, in fact transcending, his discrete visual existence, his human form, to return to the kingdom of words.

So Pasqualino finds his narrative place, his verbal heaven. But he

pays dearly for his discovery of a narrative substance. His achievement is shot through with dualism; so much so, in fact, that the final
characteristic of *Seven Beauties* is that it is, through Pasqualino's
agency, the essence of narrative by dualism. *Seven Beauties* in
many ways expresses the ancient fear of images as events that
threaten a verbally established order, a "logical" mode of thought,
even when that order is totally powerless to narrate a vision of a new
man. Narrative analogues of the central dualism of *Seven Beauties*
are readily found in the unresolved conflicts created by the initial
presence of a black-and-white sequence that only subsequently—
and in the end inconsequentially—gives way to color; in the prece-
dence of the static—Hitler's and Mussolini's initial images as well as
Pasqualino's last—over the moving images; in the emphasis on a
dominant image—again Hitler's and Mussolini's but eventually
Pasqualino's—and in the concomitant scorn for the common image,
especially the girl's; and in the actions of an individual image (Pasqualino's) who is in point of fact never an individual but a member
of "the ones," all of whom are trapped in the vast deterministic
machine of global conflict—trapped in that most anonymous of narratives, history.

The narrative model that discloses new possibilities for
Pasqualino—and for the movie itself—can create little more than a
conflict between narrative alternatives, a narrative "either/or."
Clearly segregated, the potentially liberating narrative model is
pure. It perishes precisely because of its purity, because of its incapacity to grow outside its own delimiting boundaries. There is
thus the mere promise of the new *within* the courtroom sequence,
appearing roughly halfway through the action and remaining a
bright, yet hopelessly isolated, fragment of narration. Since the
living image is never presupposed as a narrative force but is only
(perhaps even incidentally) introduced as a regenerative possibility,
Seven Beauties can never go beyond the mere suggestion that images, as the sole agents of life in the movie's own world, can beget an
immanent divinity, a divinity that is more beneficent, more human,
more *moral* than that metaphysical, otherworldly one whose
superiority Pasqualino—in all the irony of his narrative being—
nevertheless proclaims.

In this way the humanistic importance of *Seven Beauties* resides,
no doubt paradoxically, in the sort of perversity through which it

consistently denies its own possibilities for growth as a cinematic narrative. Few movies, if any, have mastered such a feat with more thoroughness, indeed with more genius. For the narrative dilemma in *Seven Beauties* is an expression of a crisis in values. The crisis may at first appear to remain safely in the realm of esthetics. But the crisis has moral consequences: it reveals the predicament not of one moviemaker but of a civilization that is profoundly aware of the death of its archaic narrative commitments yet on the whole remains afraid to explore the moral options of cinematic narration.

3

To the Threshold
of the New Narrative
BLOWUP

*Life is in the transitions as much as in the
terms connected; often, indeed, it seems to be
there more emphatically, as if our spurts and
sallies forward were the real firing-line of the
battle, were like the thin line of flame advancing
across the dry autumnal field which the farmer
proceeds to burn.*

WILLIAM JAMES

Within the consideration of the growth of cinematic values that
forms the central concern of this book, *Seven Beauties* is as anach-
ronistic and obsolescent a movie as there can possibly be. But its
very obsolescence, its narrative abnegation, is its greatest value.
Therefore inasmuch as *Seven Beauties*, like all movies of consequence, offers itself to the further examination of values inherent in
its own narrative deed, we find in it a clear summons to the exploration of an alternative narrative. Such an alternative narrative can
illustrate the growth of cinematic values beyond *Seven Beauties'*
own narrative crisis. In the case of *Blowup*, the alternative narrative
is present almost a decade before *Seven Beauties*.[1]

In the broadest possible sense, that which in *Seven Beauties* is an
unresolvable narrative dilemma is, in the case of *Blowup*, a narrative tension. This narrative tension in *Blowup* is generally speaking

created by a conflict of narrative possibilities as pronounced as that of *Seven Beauties*. But the narrative tension is ultimately a power that promotes its own resolution; it is a division that eventually succeeds in generating unity.

The tension in *Blowup* is basically produced by two contrasting modes of narration. One of these modes can be referred to as cinematic. In its most fundamental form it can be summed up as the actions and events that operate independently of the movie's central figure, the photographer.[2] The second of the two modes can be termed "photographic." It creates a narrative contrast to the cinematic mode by operating within it in a fashion that, for the most part, runs counter to the operations of the cinematic mode. Thus, unlike Pasqualino in *Seven Beauties*, the protagonist in *Blowup* is not the measure of the world in which he performs his narrative feat.

Pasqualino begins and ends his narration, framing it, as it were, with his cyclical attainment of an "imperishable" identity. The photographer, on the other hand, enters a world that announces its existence without reliance on a narrative persona. At the end he quite literally disappears from, or rather, *in* that world, while the world continues, however briefly, to be present as the last event on the screen. The photographer's most elementary function is therefore to generate narrative tension, to live, throughout much of the story, "against the beat," to use his own words, of the cinematic mode.

The life of the photographer is from the beginning characterized by narrative passion. He is impelled by an urge to change, to grow, and to express the creation of that change and that growth. Pasqualino, by contrast, has no such narrative passion. His instinct to live is more properly a narrative will, which amounts to his obstinate longing for a permanent and altogether abstract identity regardless of any and all creative events brought forth by the world.

Examples of the photographer's narrative passion are even more numerous than are those of Pasqualino's monotonous repetition of his will to live. For example, in just one brief scene, at the restaurant with Ron, the photographer changes his mind about the ending of the book of photographs, saying he's "got something fab for the end"; he says that he is "going off London" because "it doesn't do anything" for him; he later says, looking at the tall blonde who could be one of his models, "I'm fed up with those bloody bitches"; and then, almost immediately afterward, he wishes he had "tons of money," for "then," he says, he would "be free." Narrative passion is the keynote of the photographer's life.

But the greater fact about him is that for all his narrative passion he lacks the method to enact the fulfillment of that passion. It is accordingly this narrative passion which, lacking a complementary method emerging from the photographer's own actions, generates the narrative tension in *Blowup.*

So much for the fundamental narrative outcomes of *Blowup* and *Seven Beauties* and for the basic difference between the narrative functions of the protagonists. Some further differences, however, need to be noted and briefly commented upon in order to clarify further the narrative model in terms of which *Blowup* will be examined. These differences reside in the functions of color, motion, and the image. (Note that it is the differences rather than the similarities between the two movies and their protagonists which will be emphasized here.)

Color. The most immediately obvious difference between *Seven Beauties* and *Blowup* is that in *Blowup* color is directly presupposed as a narrative fact. In *Seven Beauties* the introduction of color is mediated by the opening montage. *Blowup* begins with an expanse of green grass that covers the entire screen and ends with what for all practical purposes is the same expanse of luxuriant green.[3] Therefore all events in *Blowup*, including the life of the photographer himself, come to form an intrinsic relation with this "given" world of color. There will nevertheless be throughout *Blowup* an expression of an underlying narrative tension in terms of the relation between the world of color and the black-and-white mode of seeing that belongs almost exclusively to the photographer.[4] During this chapter, when not directly stated, the world of color announced as the first event in *Blowup* will be referred to as the "public," the "organic," and the "given" (in addition to the "cinematic") world. The black-and-white narrative mode of the photographer will be referred to as the "private," the "artificial," and the "controlled" (in addition to the "photographic") world.[5] The same terms will be applied, where relevant, to the world of motion and to the static world, respectively. It is enough for now to single out the role of color as a fundamental event that throughout discloses the growth of cinematic values in *Blowup*.[6]

Motion. Behind the outline of the transparent words of the credits that are eventually superimposed on the green expanse, there appears a "happening." Dressed in a multicolored go-go outfit, a girl dances on the corner of a rooftop. A crowd watches. Early in the credit sequence there is in center foreground a (not "the") photographer holding his camera over the heads of other spectators. Thus one color (green) begets a polychromatic event, an event in which the central image, both celebrant and celebrated, moves, and in which moreover a photographer participates. Even the "Blowup" of the title explodes almost entirely out of the screen, briefly revealing more of the action that it had but a moment earlier concealed. From the beginning of *Blowup*, then, motion is no mere random physical activity. It is, at least potentially, a source of change, and constitutes in many cases the direct disclosure of the creative transformations and transitions that propel the action. As regards the photographer in his relation to a world of motion, it will be sufficient for now to mention, as a sort of prelude, that he strains the narrative tension. He freezes motion.

The image. Both color and motion are inherent in the image. Color, motion, and the image are, obviously, one indivisible event so far as the cinematic world itself goes. The life of images generates the activities of the movie camera (or of Antonioni's presiding imagination, if you will). But in a radically different manner the life of images also generates those narrative activities of the photographer which account for narrative tension. It cannot be sufficiently emphasized that narrative tension is generated because the photographer does not see the integration of color and motion in the image. And his mode of seeing denies not only color and motion, but also the potentialities for autonomous growth inherent in the moving image. Yet it is precisely in this sense that *Blowup* becomes a narrative of possibilities and above all of visual possibilities.[7] It is in many ways the quintessential story of the possibilities of seeing the image. The terms *ambiguity, ambivalence,* and *indeterminacy,* used by some critics in relation to the visual aspects of *Blowup*, represent nothing more than a negative way of looking at the movie as an open-ended narrative.[8]

The model that exemplifies the narrative tension in *Blowup* is found in one continuous action, though this action can be seen as a three-part narrative structure. The romp with the nymphs, which is the central event in the narrative model, is framed, as it were, by the photographer's two encounters with black-and-white images, one just before the entrance of the nymphs, the other just after they leave.

The sequence with the nymphs is the key model of the *dissolution* of narrative tension in *Blowup*, because in the context in which it takes place—that is, in the midst of the photographer's obsession with his peculiar mode of narration—the nymphs are liberating.[9] Irrepressible, they free the photographer from his preoccupation with the changeless and the static. Stark naked soon enough, they playfully free him from his analytic mode of thought, from his need to uncover a more telling image from the enlargement of a part of a whole image. (In this way they create a contrast with the girl, whose undressing is a last resort in her effort to get the photographer to give her the pictures he took at the park. Thus as she takes off her clothes the girl creates mystery for the photographer: what is it about those photographs that makes the girl prostitute herself for them?) Colorful and innocent, the nymphs offer the photographer a refreshing respite from his obsession with intellectualizing and interpreting the black-and-white image in which only evil lurks. Spontaneous, they lure him away from the world of artifice that enslaves him, as well as from his self-centered insistence on mastery over the private world. Free from identity, they are the agents for a life of individuality where the permanence of the ego is of negligible importance in relation to individual actions. Essentially amoral, they entice him away from his ethical concerns, and eventually they quite literally involve him in an act the "end" of which signals the birth of a positive morality, of a morality that begins to unfold in terms of the lessening of narrative tension and culminates in the photographer's assimilation by the cinematic world.

For the purposes of this chapter it will be best to give a clear, full, and perforce mechanical description of the entire sequence before commenting more upon its import as the clarifying model in *Blowup*.

Shortly after the photographer confronts the blow-ups of a man lurking behind the fence and of the hand holding the gun (in the further enlargement of a section of the fence), he telephones Ron. The photographer is excited. He thinks he has clarified the mystery which the girl, by insisting on having the pictures, has led him to inquire into. On the phone, he narrates the story of the blow-ups as follows: "Ron? Something fantastic's happened. Those photographs in the park—fantastic! Somebody was trying to kill somebody else. I saved his life. Listen, Ron, there was a girl. Ron, will you listen! What makes it so fantastic. . . ." He is interrupted in mid-sentence by a ring at the door and asks Ron to "hang on."[10]

When the photographer opens the door, the two nymphs, who obviously have been leaning against it, stumble into the private world. The blonde one says to the photographer, "You weren't expecting us, were you?" He responds with a terse no. Offscreen, after his initial irritation at this invasion of his photographic domain, he asks them, in a lighter mood, if they can "manage to make a cup of coffee" between them. The nymphs run up the stairs to the kitchen, giggling. From below, the camera sees their leotard-covered legs almost all the way up to their buttocks. The blonde wears yellow tights, the brunette shocking-pink ones. The blonde's minidress is light blue and olive green with an orange hem; the brunette's is white, light blue, and green. The photographer comes onscreen and follows slowly up the stairs.

In the kitchen, the photographer asks the brunette, "What's your name?" Then, uninterested in the formalities of an identity he says, "Ah, forget it. What's the use of a name? What do they call you in bed?" Insulted, the brunette replies, "I only go to bed to sleep." The photographer looks at her quizzically. He has received an unexpectedly innocent answer to his cynical question.

He suddenly remembers that he had been talking with Ron and dashes out of the kitchen. The camera doesn't follow the photographer; it stays in the kitchen with the nymphs, looking at them as they try to listen to the photographer's offscreen conversation. The phone line is dead, however, and they hear only the faint "hellos" of the photographer as he tries to reestablish the connection with Ron.

The nymphs have now entered a room with colorful dresses on a rack. Soon the blonde settles on one of the dresses she would like to try, takes off her own, and is for a moment bare-topped before she dons the fashionable dress that she doesn't zip up. The photographer comes in and startles the nymphs. The brunette escapes the

precarious moment by rushing out of the room and back to the
kitchen to tend to the hissing coffeepot. The blonde and the photographer are by themselves. Approaching her, the photographer grabs
one strap of the dress and pulls it down. The blonde, in a panic,
ducks under the clothes rack so that it is between her and the
photographer. The photographer grabs the entire rack, pulls it
down, and stepping over it moves toward the blonde. He grabs her
by the hair, hurting her, and pulls her toward him. Unable to free
herself, now on her knees, the blonde, who is naked from the waist
up, bites the photographer on the hand.

The brunette appears at the door. The blonde tells the photographer that the brunette has "a better figure than me," and both
approach the brunette and trap her at the door. The romp begins
when the blonde pulls the brunette down on the floor to take off her
dress. As they frolic on the floor among the colorful dresses there is
a close-up of the photographer. He laughs and claps his hands,
delighting but not actively participating in the spontaneous strip-
tease act. Finally, when both nymphs are stripped from the waist
up, they dash into the studio. The photographer follows, but he
doesn't run.

In the studio the blonde grabs the lavender backdrop paper and
unrolls it all to the floor. After a while, the photographer appears
and begins forcibly to remove the blonde's yellow tights and then
helps her take the shocking-pink ones off the brunette. The nymphs
are now totally naked. Suddenly the blonde pulls the photographer
down into the fray and both nymphs begin to undress him. He
resists, but it is only a perfunctory resistance, for the scene ends
with the three of them laughing and screaming, enveloped by the
crumpled lavender backdrop paper.

There is a silence. The camera pans down from the translucent
polyethylene window cover. The nymphs' backs are to the camera.
They are already dressed. They kneel on each side of the photographer, dressing him. The photographer awakens, sitting up on the
floor. He stares intently at something far away in another part of the
studio. He stands up and begins to walk slowly toward what he sees,
barely blinking, barely acknowledging the presence of the nymphs.
He continues to walk ahead, staring intently at the black-and-white
stills that have attracted his attention.

The camera now sees him from behind two of the blow-ups

clipped on the beam. Engrossed in what he sees, he picks up the magnifying glass, and the camera then sees him looking intently at the enlargement in which the girl stands over the dead man's body by the bush.[11] More specifically, the photographer looks at the part of the enlargement in which the upright form of the girl and the horizontal body of the dead man produce an L-shaped image.

As an afterthought, it seems, remembering that they are still there, he tells the nymphs, "All right, let's move. Out!" Dejected, the blonde says, "You haven't taken any photographs." The photographer tells her that he is too tired and that it is their fault; he promises, but only as a way of ridding himself of them, that he will take their photos tomorrow. "Tomorrow!" he screams a second time. The frightened nymphs disappear, never to be seen again. The photographer continues to get more and more involved with the image of death that he has awakened to.

As the action just described begins, the photographer is involved in an act of interpreting a sequence of images. Here the interpretive act takes on an ethical value for the photographer. What is "fantastic" about the photographs, it is implied, is that they have stopped an attempted murder. This is the event worth narrating to Ron over the telephone.

But from what can be made of the photographer's side of the conversation, Ron is not listening. Even before he is the uninterested zombie that he is much later at the party, Ron is already barely present as an audience for the photographer's story. The photographer must demand that Ron "listen." This demand shows above all that the photographer—having to rely as he does throughout on someone or something (on Patricia, later again on Ron, and finally on his own camera) to confirm the truth of his vision—is already beginning to feel the profound isolation caused by his private and controlled way of seeing the natural world. It is no cliché to say that the photographer cannot communicate. For even at this early stage, in all his ethical enthusiasm, he cannot make the "truth" of his interpretation *common*. And this failure of communication is all the more obvious, and all the more pathetic, when it is borne in mind that the photographer already thinks of images as means to the end of verbal narration. The image—even the abstract, still, black-and-white image—narrates nothing by itself. Whether he sees them at the park or in his private world, images are no more than a *medium* (in the formal, logical sense of a mediating term) between a passive, reflective consciousness and the consciousness' own penchant for verbally narrating the "truth" as well as the truth's "ethical" consequences. Such a penchant amounts to a desire to understand rationally and thus to reduce analytically whatever intrinsic value images may possess so as to demonstrate the validity of a hypothesis established a priori and thereupon to report the findings of such an abstractive pursuit.[12]

The truth of images, however, being at most a matter of experiential temporal relations, can never yield a final logical conclusion. It is therefore of slight consequence that the photographer's interpretive narration is incomplete as a result of the nymphs' intrusion. Of course the photographer reports a conclusion from half his visual evidence. Also, he will interpret the image differently twice more before movie's end. But what is crucial to note for now is that—even in the world that promotes the image's control—there is established the pattern of the denial of a mode of thought that insists that the truth of a visual encounter can be categorically elicited and demonstratively proved.

The implicit denial of demonstrative induction as a mode of narration becomes an explicit affirmation of the powers of cinematic energies the very instant the nymphs interrupt the photographer's conversation. The nymphs are not "expected." Their entrance alone therefore constitutes no less than an invasion—by the organic world of color and motion—of the kingdom where visual control as well as intellectual expectations of the image are the entrenched narrative ways. (Indeed, so fraught with novelty is this invasion that the blonde bursts into the private world backward. Color in motion, not a recognizable face, initiates the action).

But not only do the nymphs liberate the photographer from his schizoid relation to the images of the natural world, they also free him to see a radically different narrative alternative. After all, they come into his world to be seen. Indeed, their return to his private world after they have been kicked out and insulted once before is clear evidence that they are the bearers of a narrative passion all their own. Like the hopefuls at Fellini's casting office, the nymphs offer the photographer a vision of his "need" for them—of his need to be freed from his obsession with the still black-and-white image after the fashion of Fellini's eventual imaginative release from the images of Mastroianni and G. Mastorna. Thus it is not important that the nymphs are disappointed because their photographs are never taken. What is important, on the contrary, is that their photographs cannot be taken.[13] For from the beginning of the sequence the nymphs are beyond the photographer's narrative ken. They are beyond intellectualization or classification or analysis or control or artifice. The nymphs are never those "bloody bitches" that the photographer is "fed up" with. Nor are they "beautiful girls" that he "looks at" and "that's that." They are not, in sum, the objects of his visual ego. And because they are not, they force him to participate in a completely new and different way of seeing. Since, unlike all the other models, the nymphs are nonprofessional images, that is, not subjected to the photographer's dictates, they deny him his own "professional" way of seeing while simultaneously instructing him in a new one. And since, unlike the girl, they want to be seen, they deny mystery to the image and actively clarify their creative role as embodiments of the cinematic world.

Moreover, the nymphs successfully liberate the camera from having to attend persistently to those photographic images that cannot, stretch as they might, extend the life of the world that the cinematic imagination has announced as the given. Accordingly, the camera delights in looking from below at the nymphs when they run upstairs to the kitchen. It is, by contrast, only mildly interested in the photographer as he follows up the stairs. When the photographer runs out of the kitchen to renew his phone call, the camera stays in the kitchen with the nymphs, uninterested in whatever verbal narrative the photographer may want to continue on the phone.

For the moment oblivious of the photographer, the camera then attends to the nymphs as they admire the colorful dresses. By the time the photographer comes onscreen to find the blonde trying on the dress, both his egocentric ethical exuberance (expressed to Ron when he says, "I saved his life"), and his urge to narrate it have disappeared. Here the photographer enters a world that has become cinematic. Uncontrolled by the photographer, it is colorful, dynamic, whole, and thoroughly innocent. It exhibits none of the heaviness of thought about black-and-white images that so weighs the photographer down.

Accordingly, the fundamental narrative import of the photographer's romp with the nymphs is that here for the first time in *Blowup* narrative tension gives way to narrative unity. As the organic world incarnate, the nymphs lure the photographer into the action. *They* initiate the action; and *they* carry it to its consummation—both physical and spiritual—without the photographer's substantial identity as such ever once coming into play as a narrative force enacting the liberating action. The "objects"—new, scintillating, alluring—live, narrate the "subject." They appropriate it as the object of their narrative act. They reshape the photographer's vision, and, what is equally momentous, they make him an image of the cinematic world. (One of the photographer's essential narrative modes, to be examined later, entails seeing without being seen.) In a far more creative way than any of the other models could ever hope for, the nymphs become *living* models or embodiments of the spirit of generation and birth that belongs as a whole to the cinematic world.

It is their cinematic life that the photographer impulsively wants to control. But beginning with the scene with the blonde in the dressing room and ending with the last scene of the romp, the photographer quickly outgrows his wish to control the uncontrollable, passes briefly into a "voyeuristic" phase, and finally becomes an active participant in the action—all, it stands repeating, without ever consciously or subjectively *willing* to do so.

Consistent with his way of seeing the images of his private world as objects that passively submit to his whims, the photographer tears away the blonde's dress and then pulls her by the hair. Bare-topped and now on her knees, she is momentarily at the mercy of the photographer, who stands over her. But then she bites him on the hand, rebelling against his pretentious mastery over her.

When the brunette appears at the door of the dressing room the blonde screams, "She's got a better figure than me." The mock-fight ensues, its only discernible object—if one can or even ought to be ascribed to it—being to show, for the photographer's delight, the stripped-down image, which is to say the colors of the flesh in the form of a moving "figure" such as the black-and-white photographic film can never hope to register. Here the photographer becomes a "voyeur." Yet his is not the furtive eye that it was at the doss house or at the park. And his is not that furtive eye quite simply because he does not use his camera to freeze the action or, as is also his wont, to mask his eye as ego and intellectualize the living event before him. Instead he laughs and claps his hands and urges the nymphs on. His delight is nothing less than the natural delight in the unmediated act of seeing, an act which itself insists on and accordingly begets more visual action.

The nymphs run from the dressing room, chasing each other. The blonde tears and pulls down the roll of lavender backdrop paper. This paper, which the photographer had so daintily pulled down so as to have a background for the girl to pose in front of is now the color in which the consummation of the liberating action takes place. Color is not now a decoration; it is a functional event increasing the life of the action as the action itself continues to increase at its unrestrainable pace to the moment of unity between the private and the public world.

More than a desultory episode providing comic relief and much more than a scene of "insignificant dalliances" (as one critic has called it),[14] the sequence with the nymphs is the central event that locates the source of the photographer's possible salvation. The "unexpected" invasion of the private sanctum is complete. The photographer, an arrogant alienated ego, has been stripped bare of his self-centered antipathy to the natural narrative powers and has ceased to be an ego resisting existence as an image. The revelation of his image is thus not only a physical event but a spiritual event as well. The tensions have disappeared. The new, the cinematic mode of narration is there, triumphant. Whether or not the photographer can extend the life of such a triumph remains as a central topic of discussion.

For now it is as accurate to say that in the world of color the photographer "dies" to be merely *re*born to his photographic ways as it is to say that out of the same world of color he is born to enact a process of narrative growth that begins with the vision of the triply-dead image (i.e., a black-and-white still of a dead man). On the one hand, his awakening to see the photograph where the girl stands by the dead man signals his recurrent obsession with knowledge about the photographic image; it marks the heightening of narrative tension. On the other, his awakening is the first act, born of the con-

summation of his passion in the cinematic world, which initiates the
death of the photographic mode (and thus by extension the birth of
the cinematic life).

In any case, it is crucial to see that upon his awakening to the
image of death a union between the photographer and that image is
established. The awakening therefore is properly speaking both itself and its possibilities, initiating, in the context within which those
possibilities arise, the process that clarifies the photographer's ultimate narrative condition.

Thus the possibilities that arise out of the photographer's vision of
death and out of his inseparability from the image of death generate
the beginning of a four-phase process consisting of (1) his confrontation with the image of death in the final blow-up; (2) his unmediated
encounter with the unedited and unanalyzed dead image of the man
in the public world of the park; (3) the intellectual consequences for
the photographer of the disappearance of the unedited image in the
greenness of the park; and (4) the photographer's own disappearance in the green expanse at the end.

Certainly the steady annihilation of the photographic mode is
present in these phases of the process, though in precisely what
form it is at this point difficult to determine. The rest of this chapter
will be structured around the examination of each of the four phases
of the birth-death process in as full a relation to the whole of *Blowup*
as possible. Throughout, the sequence just attended to remains at
the center, a vision of the possibilities for the photographer's own
"tomorrow" and, most important, for all the cinematic tomorrows
that a careful study of *Blowup*, not to mention *Blowup* itself, can
beget.

Perhaps one of the most obvious similarities between the way the
photographer sees his private world and the way he sees the public
world can be found in his insistence on creating visual perspective in
both. One of the chief attributes of the photographic mode of narration is the imposition of perspective on what is seen.[15]

For example, the session with the model begins with the arrangement of the colorful feathers. The feathers occupy the immediate left foreground and extend outward "in space" to form a
point in the center of the screen (or of the still camera's viewfinder).
The model, dressed in black, stands at the end of this point created

by color. The backdrop paper behind her is also black. There is nothing beyond her that attracts the eye or that relates her to a greater visual world. The model is therefore the dominant image of the *mise en scène*, occupying the point of infinity in it. Color is mere decoration, artifice, in the foreground. Its most "valuable" function is to point to the colorless image in infinite space. Eventually, when the photographer continues the session by moving closer to the model with the 35mm camera, he is in fact moving into that perspective world. Then he sits on top of the model, who is stretched out on the floor. He dominates the dominant image in the dominant point of infinity. His celebrated photographic orgasm (highlighted by the photographer's "Yes, yes, yes!") is really an orgasm with the conceptually controlled image in infinity.

Regarding the photographic session with the model, it is also significant that after the orgasmic moment the photographer gets up and walks away from the model. She is now in the foreground, exhausted. Equally exhausted, he almost instinctively walks *into* a farther point, plopping down on the sofa in the background, becoming the new point of perspective. (Not only does he create and dominate the point through his way of seeing, he also tends to insist on being seen as just such a point.) The photographer's "yes!" is not so much an affirmation of visual delight as it is of his success in forcing his point of view, his perspective, to submit to his dictates—dictates that themselves have their origin in an intellectual point of view.

What is "born" of this visual orgasm—and indeed established as a major component of the photographic narrative mode—is a way of seeing in which perspective is a presupposed condition of the image. And what is also "born"—and established as a major force in the photographer's narrative arsenal—is his egocentric control of the point of perspective. From his isolated point of view he attends to another point, all to the exclusion of the rest of the life in the frame. Accordingly, the actions that allow him to draw the proper gestures and expressions from the submissive model will later find their more momentous counterpart in the photographer's feverish insistence on eliciting the meaning, the "point" of the image of death.

Another clear instance of the photographer's affinities with perspective is evident in the second *mise en scène* with the five models. This time the models wear dresses that are more colorful.

Yet ironically, the more colorful the dress, the farther away the
photographer has positioned the model who wears it; so that the first
model, ever so consistently with the "fashion" of the private world,
wears a black-and-white dress. Thus color is again sacrificed for the
sake of perspective. After the camera pans right and stops over a
shoulder shot that aligns it with the photographer's camera, the
models are seen divided by the vertical edges of the smoked glass
panes that are arranged in a receding diagonal row across the screen,
each pane overlapping the right hand portion of the next. The effect
is of course one of depth. But precisely for the sake of this effect, half
the images are seen through a glass darkly. Moreover, perspective
robs the images of their motion, creating, as it always does, a still
point. Thus divided, robbed of their motion, and arranged so that
the last and least visually particularized model in the row is what the
"sequence" ends in, the actual photographs need not be (as they
never are) seen. They have been so maliciously controlled as to
make the net difference between the actual images and the photographs zero. And what is just as vicious, at the end of the session the
photographer orders the models to close their eyes. "And stay like
that," he commands. "It's good for you." His control over his images
extends over their own visual capacities. Thus he proclaims himself
master over the models, over the images of perspective, by blinding
them that he may be undisputed lord of the visible.

In these contexts perspective is a thoroughly intellectual, indeed
a Platonic, way of seeing. Perspective discloses its full narrative
significance in terms that are precisely those that endow the image
with onerous transcendental attributes.[16] It leads to the visual
preoccupation with the superior images found in so many of the
works of the Italian masters.[17] It finds its most elaborate theoretical
exposition in Leonardo's writings, as exemplified in the following
definitions:

If you extend the lines from the edges of each body as they converge you
will bring them to a single point. . . .
Perspective is nothing more than a rational demonstration applied to the
consideration of how objects in front of the eye transmit their image to it, by
means of a pyramid of lines. The *Pyramid* is the name I apply to the lines
which, starting from the surface and edges of each object, converge from a
distance and meet in a single point.

Perspective is a rational demonstration, by which we may practically and clearly understand how objects transmit their own image. . . .[18]

As far as the photographer's narrative inclinations go, the key terms here are "single point," "rational demonstration," and "understand[ing]." Also, it is important to note that Leonardo does not write of only one-half of the visual relation established by perspective—that is, of the "single point" as if it existed only as a property of the image. He refers equally to the projection of a rational demonstration, a concept imposed *on* the image of perspective by what implicitly amounts to a consciousness outside the image. The two "perspectives" are not complementary; they are manifestations of each other.

Ultimately, then, when all of his infantile outbursts during the photographic sessions are done with, when perspective is no longer a whimsical visual preference, and when visual arrogance is no mere childish impulse, the photographer's shocking confrontation with the visual point of death arouses in him the sobering urgency *to understand* the visual point that he sees and *to demonstrate rationally* the "real" existence of that single visual point, a single visual point which is not only "the body's," but also his very own.

For this reason, there is within the photographer himself an aspect of that greater, more pervasive narrative tension that he creates in his relation to the cinematic world. True, the photographer wants to change. But his narrative passion has its source in an "I." The ego becomes the part of the photographer that at once expresses and holds back his narrative passion. The ego is his perspective, his narrative point of view. His ego and his eye, his self-concept and his mode of seeing, are for all practical purposes one and the same. Both resist unity with the cinematic world; both resist change. This means that the photographer's vision bears such a high degree of abstraction—has become so inseparable from his ego—that he comes to act as if he is not an image of the cinematic world but a pure ego. An anti-image all his own, then, his "image" serves him as a disguise for an illusory self-concept which in turn allows him to ascribe an imperishable "reality" to his ego.

As a result, the photographer has a tendency to try to hide himself in a point created by perspective. (Thus he runs to the end of the street alongside the doss house; yet the camera, following the visual lead of one of the mummers, readily sees him. Also, in the high-angle shot, as he sits behind the desk, he buttons up his shirt, visibly embarrassed that even in his conceptual point of safety the nymphs—extensions of the cinematic powers even this early in the story—can see him.) Or else he is clearly irritated when he finds no image of a perspective point (when he drives into his own street after trying to follow the blond man). But his aim at invisibility and his fascination with perspective never bear more significance nor are they ever more strongly asserted than at the park.

From inside the park the camera sees the photographer, who is out on the street, as a small point in the background.[19] The gate in the middle ground frames him. In the foreground the four trees frame the gate, two on each side, so that the gate gives further depth to the photographer's image. From the beginning he is singled out as the anti-image which, armed with its rational tool, the still camera, invades the organic world. It is no mere coincidence that the photographer is dressed in black and white (black jacket and white trousers). Even as he enters the world of color he cannot slough off his qualities as an abstract image.

Nor is it mere coincidence that once inside the park the first thing he trains his camera on is the tennis court. In the world of color—the green of the grass and of the swaying treetops and the white and the pink of the flowers—the first image the photographer gets interested in is the fenced-in, the self-divided, the geometrical, the altogether abstract, dark gray of the tennis court. In this new world of self-reproductive, self-narrating color, the photographer focuses on what is segregated from what moves and grows.

That he does not actually snap the picture of the tennis court is, however, an immediate indication that he has at least momentarily rejected the image of abstraction; so that, when after a cut he chases the pigeons on the ground and snaps their pictures, he begins, so far as he can for now, to get in tune with the organic world. In fact, he is further lured by motion when he sees the girl leading the man up the hill. This is most obvious in the next shot, where the photographer hops, skips, and taps his feet in the air as he comes up the stairway that is flanked by fences, all the time moving toward the foreground. In all the intuitive exuberance of finding himself for once free of his inhibitive world, he naturally moves away from the background, from the fixed point, and into the foreground. And what is more, the motion that carries him away from the fixed point indicates a momentary disregard for concealing his own image. He runs so as to see more clearly, and moving, he is seen more clearly. His narrative passion coalesces, if only momentarily, with the narrative forces of the cinematic world.

But having seen the girl and the man, the photographer almost instinctively decides that he won't be seen. He jumps behind the fence and begins to take their pictures. Thus the blow-up sequence showing the assassin behind the fence need not be seen in order to establish the actions of the photographer as those of a killer. The image of the assassin in the photographer's private world is more an image of *corroborating* than of incriminating evidence. As the photographer hides, so does the assassin; as the photographer shoots to "kill," so does the assassin; and as in the end the black-and-white image of the photographer disappears in the world from which he imported the assassin's, so does the assasin's black-and-white image disappear from the frozen moment of the public world that the photographer imports into his private domain.

But the photographer's instinct to kill the image (and his resulting affinity with the assassin), is only one of the relations established in the park. Not only does the photographer look to kill, he also wants to look without being seen. Inasmuch as his egocentric narrative inclinations allow him to believe that he can be an invisible eye, the photographer already indicates his wish to die as an image of the cinematic world. Dead as an "image" that looks but does not see, he also begins to acquire strong ties with the image of the dead body.

Now what the deadly eye kills from behind the fence, from behind three different trees, and even later from the bottom of the steps, is an action which of itself involves a separation. (This act of separation between the girl and the man will become all the more pronounced through the photographer's analytical ways in his private world.) First of all, both the girl and the man are, as images, at odds with, separate from, the world of color. Both wear black and white or gray clothes. In this very elemental sense then, they are not altogether innocent of abetting the conflict between the photographic and the cinematic. (Later, at the photographer's, the girl says, "My private life's already in a mess." Indeed, what she brings to the park, even in terms of her visual appearance, is her messy "private life.")

Second, the girl and the man, who are first seen (by the photographer) walking up the hill, eventually break their embrace in the meadow when the girl discovers the photographer.[20] In fact, even during the embrace it is already clear that the girl looks over her shoulder at some distant point. She ignores the man who is nearest her and looks (presumably at least) for the assassin behind the fence. In this way she in effect finds herself looking for the photographer at the point of perspective. *And since the invisible point is the one that the photographer gets engrossed in during the first half of his analytical activity, the girl not only "sees" the photographer but the photographer eventually "sees" himself as the point being looked at by the girl.*

Third and last, the act of separation culminates in an attempt to die as images, both on the part of the photographer and on the part of the girl. Seeing the photographer, the girl runs toward him, leaving the man behind. The photographer himself runs away, trying desparately to retain his invisibility. The girl accosts him near the bottom of the steps. He then turns around and begins to snap pictures of her. His impulse is clear evidence of his conviction that, even in the cinematic world, he can stop the girl's motion, can kill her with his photographic weapon.

But what is equally important is that the girl herself announces a will to invisibility all her own. She orders him to "stop it"; then, so as not to be seen, she holds her hand over her face. (This act is what will later become, when fully translated into the photographic mode, the "see-no-evil" photograph.) She then pulls at the camera by the strap and bites him on the hand to make him let go of it. (This act of biting invites comparison with the bite that the blonde gives the photographer. The blonde bites him so as to continue her obstreperous action. The girl bites him in order to bring all action to a "stop.") Moreover, in asserting that the park is "a public place" and that in such a place "everyone has the right to be left in peace," she further singles herself out as an agent of narrative tension. She wants to keep her image private (or "to be left in peace") in a world that, by her own admission, can't conceal her privately motivated actions. And when the photographer, in all the triumphant pride that consumes him as possessor of both his weapon and his prey, cynically, cruelly, says, "Don't let's spoil everything, we've only just met," the girl replies, "No, we haven't met. You've never seen me."

"You've never seen me." These are the last words in the park sequence. And because the photographer returns to the park (twice) only in his role as an intellectual obsessed with a mystery, the girl's words are in point of fact an apocalyptic pronouncement on the photographer's one and only spontaneous adventure into the cinematic world. More than a self-contained negation of the possibilities for the fulfillment of the photographer's narrative passion in the public world, the girl's words are an ominous prelude to the broader narrative consequences suffered by the photographer as a result of his invasion of the organic and the colorful. The girl thus foretells the disappearance of the blond mystery man in the streets of London as well as that of the blow-ups from the photographer's studio. She moreover foretells the photographer's admission to Patricia that he "didn't see" the man killed. She announces the disappearance of "the body" in the park, as well as of her own image, right before the photographer's eyes, under the Permutit sign. Her last words at the park find their final expression in the photographer's verbal admission of the disconcerting nature of his narrative mode and of its thorough inadequacy to satisfy his narrative passion, when he replies, "Nothing," in response to Ron's question: "What did you see in that park?" But then, precisely because the girl's words are a first indication of the moral, esthetic, and narrative inadequacy of the photographic mode, and precisely because they so inform all the visual transitions and transformations that are to occur, they also announce the photographer's own disappearance into the world of color. His disappearance is no less than his final visual "beat" as "a photographer" just before his image is assimilated by the cinematic world.

"You've never seen me." The girl's last words are not exclusively a subtle preface of things to come for the photographer. They are also, in fact, primarily, an expression of her own wish, altogether analogous to the photographer's, to be invisible. Thus, after the photographer succeeds in retaining possession of his camera, the girl runs away into the distance. She is framed by the fences on either side of the steps. The photographer compulsively begins to snap more pictures. The girl stops by the bush, which is the last point in the horizon. From his unchanged point of view the photographer continues to shoot, failing, for all that he will know for a long while, to see the dead body for the girl. But when the girl disappears over the hill it is the torso of the dead man that becomes quite literally the fixed point, becomes the ultimate image of perspective even here, now, before the photographer sees it for the first time after his encounter with the nymphs. In the end more capable than the photographer, the girl succeeds in becoming invisible. For the measure of her success is not that she is somehow better at concealing her image, but that her image becomes relatively unimportant to the photographer—unimportant, that is, in relation to the image of death that haunts him.

The act of separation is more "complete" than would appear at first glance. Once the photographer becomes fully one with the dead image that he fails to see, there is no real difference between the girl's separation from the man in order to stop the photographer and the girl's separation from the photographer as she runs away from his camera and toward the point where the man already lies dead. That after the sequence at the park the photographer says to Ron that the pictures in the park were "very peaceful, very still" (this being his first interpretation of what he saw) or that at his own flat he says to the girl that "the light was very beautiful in the park [that] morning," are nothing but consummately ironic indications of his blindness. For the upshot of his venture into the world of color is that he has perversely succeeded in turning the inherently cinematic into the essentially photographic.

It should therefore come as no surprise that the photographer's narrative fate ultimately hinges upon his obsession with a *part*—and a dead one at that—of the whole cinematic world. His every inclination is to seize a part of an image and turn it into the whole. Of course, to be obsessively concerned with perspective as the *sine qua non* of the image is to be irredeemably engrossed in the importance of a part; it is to look for the "chief image" in the part. It is almost superfluous, then, to say that to live as though perspectivism were the exclusive way of seeing is, to the degree the visual world will allow, to live teleologically; it is to live in search of the ultimate meaning of a part only after the ego has ascribed an overweening importance to such a part. Permanence is the reward for the ego's obsession with the partial image.

The photographer's impulsive predisposition to analyze the image so as to reach its essence is best and most significantly illus-

trated in the analytical arrangement and blow-up process, both before and after the romp with the nymphs. But such a process is more
properly speaking the intensification of the photographer's pervading impulse to control fragments of the whole visual experience. The
airplane propeller, the Go Away sign, and the guitar neck are the
most obvious fragments that he "shores against" a world that is by
nature organic. All of these have an importance for the photographer that is transitory (though their function within the larger context of the action is not merely incidental).[21] Thus when the propeller arrives, the photographer has all but forgotten that he had
bought it earlier that morning. The Go Away sign flies off the rear
seat of the Rolls and the photographer never seems to notice. And
no sooner is he out of the Ricky Tick than he drops the neck of the
guitar.

His flat is filled with fragments to which he has obviously attached himself with the same frenzied cupidity that leads him to
possess the propeller or the guitar neck, but which have nonetheless
become so much bric-a-brac cluttering his private world. The
marblelike heads at each end of the sofa and those by the garage
door, one of a "turbaned turk" and one, in color, of a woman, are
examples of his bent to possess what is not whole.

Moreover, these physical fragments find an important parallel in
the photographer's own inability to finish even the most elementary
of acts. He doesn't, for instance, finish the beer that Patricia serves
him or the meal he orders at the restaurant or the drinks he pours
for himself at his place or the cigarettes he lights up. Most of his
telephone calls somehow manage to get cut off. He doesn't complete
the photographic session with the models. And the motions of both
the frogman and the skydiver in his photographs are arrested in
midair, so that not even his images complete the act that they set
out to perform. He gets hopelessly sidetracked while trying to find
the blond man and even more so when trying to follow the girl after
he sees her standing under the Permutit sign. In the threshold of his
bedroom, the anticipated love scene with the girl gets interrupted
by the arrival of the delivery boy who brings the propeller. He
cannot, and this is perhaps more important, get to the park to "take a
picture of the body." In this light, his words to the girl, after the
only phone call he receives, fully bespeak his pathetically fragmen-
tary existence. He has said to the girl that the phone call is from his

wife, but then he says: "She isn't my wife, really. We just have some kids. No, no kids. Not even kids. Sometimes, though, it feels as if we had kids. She isn't beautiful, she's easy to live with. No she isn't. That's why I don't live with her. But even with beautiful girls, you, you look at them and that's that. That's why they always end up by—anyway, I'm stuck with them all day long." (This denial of any creative human relation finds its clarifying counterpart in the photographer's denial of seeing that takes place during the scene with Patricia.) All he completes are two photographic acts, one with the model, the other when he sees the final blow-up. It is certainly more than coincidence that the last words of the former act are "Yes, yes, yes!" while the final verbal reference to the latter is "Nothing." Nothingness is photography's fate in *Blowup*. And nothingness is the fate of the dissociated sensibility in *Blowup*.

Then there are the images of the antique shop, their most significant feature being that when the photographer is among them he is never in a relation to a whole image. A headless statue of a woman in neoclassical dress is in the right foreground when the photographer enters the shop the first time. In the left middle ground there are two plaster busts. As he moves inside the shop, the camera pans with him as he walks to the left of the screen and sees a group of four more busts, and then, as the camera continues to move, it sees four more. And, finally, in the left foreground, almost as if to add unity and symmetry to the camera's pan, there is a headless statue of yet another woman in neoclassical dress. Also, the landscape painting that the photographer uncovers (the whole of which is never actually seen) is concealed by three small plaster busts.

Examples of the photographer's own fragmentation as an image abound throughout. Perhaps the most important of these, singling him out as a man of the head, is the camera's view of him from behind as he looks at the first two enlargements. He is only an eyeless, bodyless head "looking," from the sofa, at the two photographs. When he sits on the rocker at Bill's, half his body is in one room, the other half in the other. Many times, as he drives his Rolls convertible, the camera shoots from such an angle that his head is cut off, as it were, by the top of the windshield. (This disjunction, incidentally, parallels that created by the girl's black neckerchief, which so neatly separates her head from her naked upper body.) And when he calls the girl on the phone, he is divided vertically by the edge of a pane of glass. When the photographer returns to the antique shop after his visit to the park, the camera sees him and the old man from inside as the two stand outside the shop. Between the photographer's and the old man's heads (all the camera sees from inside) is a Roman bust just inside the store—three heads, the living not appreciably different from the dead. So when it is borne in mind that the photographer wants to buy the antique shop, his relations to a visually fragmented world further clarify his penchant for owning even more artifice, more of that which separates him from the cinematic and the organic.

There is one part, one fragment of his life that the photographer will almost throughout not let go of; that fragment is his camera. His camera is in a brown paper bag along with the money that he so willingly parts with when he gives it to the mummers. And earlier he clutches the bag to his body when he talks to the doss house derelicts. Before he gets out of the Rolls, upon arriving at his flat, he locks it in the glove compartment. The girl's inability to wrest it from him at the park (and to steal it from his flat later on) is further evidence of the permanent value he places on his camera. And in the end, after he tosses the "nothing ball" into the "nothing tennis court" ("nothing," since the movie camera never comes back to it), he walks back to get his camera, which has been lying on the grass, and holds on to it until he altogether disappears in the green expanse. His still camera is through and through an instrument of the visual self. It is the technological counterpart of his ego.

However, it is the scene with Bill that best clarifies the pervasiveness of the photographer's desire for control of both visual and conceptual fragments, especially in relation to the manner in which such a desire unfolds throughout and even well after the blow-up sequence.

The photographer's entrance into Bill's apartment is an entrance into a private world all its own. As much as it is the domain of painting, if not more so, Bill's is the realm of criticism about the image. For all that the camera shows, Bill never paints. Thus, despite the blue and red smudges on his white T-shirt, Bill is not so much a painter as he is a man of passive intellection. He contemplates the "meaning" of a part. "That must be five or six years old," he says to the photographer while pointing at a picture on the easel. "They don't mean anything when I do them, just a mess.

Afterwards I find something to hang on to [camera closer to picture, Bill pointing to a part of the painting], like that, like that leg. Then it sorts itself out. It adds up. It's like finding a clue in a detective story." Then, turning toward the canvas sprinkled with color drops, which lies on the floor, Bill says, "Don't ask me about this one. I don't know yet."

Bill's "explication" begins demonstratively. He refers to the painting as a conceptual object, as some *thing* in need of intellectual mediation, of rational proof, so that it can be talked about. The image is a "that" outside the self. In fact, so much rational mediation is required in order to elicit the image's meaning that time itself becomes the "medium." The immediate visual event, so goes Bill's criticism, is "just a mess"; it can have no intrinsic value. But the greatest irony of Bill's intellect is that after "five or six years" of contemplative thought, the "meaning," the extraneously ascribed importance and thus the *thing to hang on to* is dictated by the supremacy of the part over the whole. And that part can only have significance in comparative terms. The part of the autonomous image (the painting) is compared to the concept of it in Bill's mind. Thus the part is not "a leg" given to immediate perception. It becomes a leg only when Bill demonstratively says it is so.

And Bill's paintings (especially the freshest ones) are objects-of-knowledge, requiring, for their necessary epistemological justification, a rational incubation that will, he hopes, hatch a meaning such as will in turn make them worthwhile to hang on to. Therefore the act of creation itself is pronounced void of value; it is on the other hand redeemed from "nonbeing" by the contemplative ego to which in the end, as in the beginning, permanence belongs as *the exclusive quality* enabling that ego to find, derivately of course, a "clue," *a word* in the fragment.

To this extent there is no doubt about the similarities between Bill's and the photographer's modes of narration about the image. The photographer's four interpretations of what he sees in the photographs of the park (and especially in those that are a part of a whole) are sufficient evidence of his inclinations to "see" rationally, of his entrenched way of looking for the aboriginal "stuff" in images in which vital cinematic constituents never figure as values. In short, Bill and the photographer share in the urge to name the ineffable and in the smugness of their classifications of the visual.

But the differences between Bill and the photographer are what make the photographer and not Bill an agent for *Blowup*'s narrative advance. To begin with, Bill has nothing whatever to do with the public world. His world is immeasurably more private than the photographer's (even if the photographer later sees him making love to Patricia). Bill's rational demonstrations can be made without any discernible recourse to the most basic kind of empirical data (such as a photograph, for instance). Most important, as both artist and critic in a thoroughly private world, Bill's pictorial and critical narrations have no ultimate human consequences. Thus, ever-possessive of the sterile integrity of his private world, he refuses to sell or give the photographer the painting. His narrative passion, if he has one, dies the instant he refuses to release the visual narrative he knows nothing of.

The photographer, on the other hand, wants to "publish" his images. He is after all putting together a book of photographs. Hence his narrative passion: his desire to change the book's ending, his initial excitement over what he sees in the park, his urge to tell Ron and Patricia about what he has seen, and so forth. And a far more crucial difference between Bill's and the photographer's modes of narration is that the photographer's images beget others. Admittedly, they do not do so through their own nature, as do movie images, but through the photographer's mediating powers. Yet in this respect alone the photographer's basic mode of narration bears more affinities to the cinematic mode of narration than Bill's. Hence too the photographer's possibilities for eventual growth in the cinematic world as opposed to Bill's "death" in his equally dead narrative world.

But despite these differences, these very important differences, there is ultimately a great similarity between Bill and the photographer. That similarity is evident in the photographer's own criticism of photographic narration. For, like Bill, the photographer will come to reflect on the meaning of a fragment of an action—in fact, on the meaning of a fragment of a fragment of an action. He will thus sever the relation with the visual mode of perception that can potentially propel him into the cinematic world, and he will altogether abandon the potentially saving power of his visual and narrative passion. Then the one fragment to which he will cling will be not his camera, but his ego. Or, more accurately, he will cling to his camera as an extension of his ego. It is the photographer's ego that ultimately allows him to point demonstratively at the image of death and to claim that what he sees and has seen has no bearing on his fragmented and thoroughly private self-concept.

As far as the two blow-up sessions themselves go, there is no question but that narrative passion, in the beginning and in the end, takes on the various guises of intellectual curiosity. At the park the photographer ignored the fact that the photos of the man and the girl concealed a story; he gave them no more importance than he did those of the antique shop or of the pigeons. ("What's so important about my bloody pictures?" he later asks the girl.) But the girl wants the photographs. She is jumpy (note how she startles when the photographer turns on a light). Her reply to the photographer's question about the importance of his "bloody pictures" is a terse "That's my business." Her "private life," she says, "[is] already in a mess. It would be a disaster . . ." Her words trail off, leaving it up to the photographer to decipher the precise possibility on which the "disaster" of her life hinges. And later she can't, as the photographer asks her to, smoke "against the beat" of the music, because, as she says, she is "nervous enough as it is." She then asks him for a drink of water. While he is away she goes for the still camera, tries to run away with it, and is caught by the photographer as she makes her way downstairs. And she is willing to go to bed with the photographer, her price being the undeveloped roll of film. The photographer, it is clear, has looked at something but has failed to see it. Toward the end of the blow-up sessions, however, intellectual curiosity is no idle pastime. Instead, curiosity becomes more properly the photographer's self-imposed demand that he reassure himself intellectually about the permanence of his own existence. Intellectual curiosity is transformed into an obsession with knowledge about the fragmented self.

The blow-up process begins, as it must, with one image. The photographer has had to cut the negatives and then to look at the positives one by one. More specifically, then, the enlargement process (from negative to 8 x 10 and from negative to 16 x 20), beginning as it does with one image, presupposes the capacity of one part of a visual action, and not of the organic narrative event to which that action inherently belongs, to clarify the assumed "mystery" of the image.

The first enlargement is of the image of the girl pulling the man by the arm. The second is an enlargement of the embrace. The most obvious feature of these two enlargements is that the human images in them are at the point of perspective. These, and especially the second one, are the images that will lead the photographer deeper into the heart of visual analysis.

But also at this moment the movie camera pans from the first to the second enlargement and then back again. Only mere conjecture would have it that the camera independently creates the sequence by initiating a relation between the stills. Only mere conjecture would have it, on the other hand, that the photographer's eyes already move from one to the other and that the camera follows the movement of his eyes. It ought to be enough to say that the movie camera both explores the photographic mode and exposes its limitations. However, it is proper to add that the camera is more than willing to explore the photographic mode to whatever extent the photographer may push it and then beyond. The first clear example of the movie camera's ability to look photographically occurs during the shooting session with the model. The jump-cuts that interrupt the fluidity of the model's motions are clear indications that the movie camera sees as though it were a still camera. Later, during the blow-up sequence, the camera zooms into the different enlargements and blow-ups. It looks hard for something which, it finally discovers, cannot a movie make (thus at once exploring photography and exhibiting its narrative limitations). Toward the end of the story, it twice pans across the tennis court, following the nothing ball that the mummers "play" with—exploring, yet again undermining, the visual "reality" of the game. And when the nothing ball is hit out of the court, the camera pans left a distance along the green expanse. If the nothing ball was nothing inside the abstract world of the tennis court, it is less than nothing outside of it.

At any rate, the act of "panning" from one enlargement to the other is the first indication the photographer has that one image alone is insignificant as a clue to the mystery he seeks to unravel. Or conversely—and this is a more momentous discovery—the photographer finds that he is looking for an action, for a sequence of events, and not for one image. He jumps off the sofa, takes down the enlargement of the embrace, and returns with a blow-up of it. He has located his narrative passion in *related images*, in a relation that is continuous, and whose continuity supplies its own transitions.

But because he of necessity seeks to unfold that action by working from the image of perspective; because the active, cinematic counterpart of those images did not want to be seen in the first place; and because his eye succeeded in turning the cinematic action into a photographic abstraction, his excitement—which is at least implicitly an excitement over the discovery of cinematic narration—is necessarily dampened because he now has to make a continuous sequence out of what he did not care to see as such when it *was* one. Therefore his only way into the "mystery" of the sequence is, ironically, through a reversion to the photographic mode, for in order to clarify the mystery that he intellectually perceives, he has to blow up the enlargements that make the sequence and thus work from a part of what is already a part. He now finds that the more he blows up those images the less concreteness, the less definition, they have.

The net result is that demonstrative interpretation increases in direct proportion to the decrease in concreteness that the blow-ups cause in the image. The more he blows them up the more mysterious they become. Thus the fundamental difficulty with the photographer's narrative passion during the blow-up sequence is that in his habituation to his photographic ways he strains the narrative tension with every blow-up, with every interpretation of the "sequence," with every addition of static image to static image which will never—*add and interpret and analyze as he might*—amount to a movie. It is not now so much that the photographer insists on seeing analytically; it is simply that he can't help it. Thus, since the images let the photographer see only more numerous (and yet less distinct) parts of themselves, a "whole" is introduced by the photographer as the ultimate "synthetic" tool. That "whole" is his ego, whose function is to impose associations among analyzed images and to find a common denominator among them that will explain them.

That his ego becomes the mediating agency acting to create a cinematic "sequence" is readily borne out in those all-important moments when the camera abandons the photographer's own visual relation to the photographs. For example, after the photographer looks at the enlargement of the embrace and runs his finger over the

girl's line of vision, the camera adopts a different angle. From behind and between two of the enlargements, the camera now sees the
photographer pour himself a glass of red wine while he looks intently at the enlargements. The photographer is the connection
between the fragments. He is what relates them. It is then that,
resuming the photographer's own relation to the photographs, the
camera sees him looking with the magnifying glass at a point in the
center of the second enlargement and marking off a small square in
it with a white wax pencil. This small square becomes the blow-up of
the fence showing the man lurking behind the fence, and it in turn
eventually becomes, after it is blown up further, the photograph of
the hand holding the gun.

The ego works its analysis from a part of a part of a part, and so
forth, the result being a narrative *reductio* that ends in the atomized
image. Of course, the other half of this modus operandi is, ironically
enough, that the selfsame ego searches for a whole story in those
atomized images. But there are no inherent cinematic transitions
from part to part; there is no narrative life in the part except what
paltry version of it is extraneously and derivately imposed by the
ego.[22] The power to make transitions is therefore the power that the
intellectual ego claims. Demonstrative analysis is only the narrative
tool employed by the intellectual ego to make transitions. But the
ego performs its "transitional" activities, it dictates changes and
relations, while simultaneously proclaiming itself incapable of
change and essentially outside the action it pretends to relate.

Ever capable of showing the photographer himself as part of a
cinematic sequence simply by moving from one image to the other
without breaks in the action and without singling out any one image
as superior, the movie camera also shows the photographer as the
"bedding" that gives a merely conceptual unity to the photographic
"mosaic." Here then is as clear an instance of narrative tension as
can be: the cinematic powers simultaneously unfold a continuous sequence and display the fatal limitations of photographic analysis.

An even more crucial instance of the way in which the photographer egocentrically establishes the relations between his photographs takes place almost immediately after he comes back with the
first blow-up of the fence. The blow-up of the embrace is already
clipped on the beam. The photographer pins the blow-up of the
fence on the adjacent wall, so that it is at right angles to the blow-up

of the embrace. The visual result is that the girl "looks" at the man behind the fence. But then the camera moves from the blow-up of the fence to the photographer and only then to the blow-up of the embrace. Once again the photographer is the bedding. Yet what happens now—and what begins to transform the function of the photographer's narrative mode—is that the ego acquires an ineluctable affinity with the visual coordinates that it "thinks" are existentially distinct from it: the photographer, standing between the two blow-ups, within the right angle that they form, is now a connecting image that has become an intrinsic part of that sequence which he believes he can remain outside of (as an ego), related merely by intellectual curiosity. In short, he may solipsistically believe that he is the measure of all things visual, but his very existence in a world of unmediated transitions, as borne out by the movie camera's activity, offers a radically different view. His image is both itself and a transition in the sequence. If he believes otherwise, and clearly he does, he but generates more narrative tension. The life and death in those images begin to undermine the photographer's self-centered aloofness when he least suspects it. The photographer finds himself being looked at by the girl, and in turn looking at the man and the girl just as the man behind the fence does.

After he fails to connect with the girl by telephone, the photographer returns to the analytic process. The process, for all the photographer knows, has yielded none of that clear-cut certainty that would have satisfied his intellectual curiosity. He has had therefore to appeal to an extraneous authority for help in narrating a complete story out of the photographs. But now, his narrative passion rekindled, he returns to the blow-up of the man behind the fence. To its immediate right, on the same wall, is the "see-no-evil" photograph of the girl. The girl hasn't given the photographer an answer during their encounters at the park or at his studio; she has made it impossible for him to get an answer from her over the telephone; and now her own frozen image also signals to him that he should look no further, that he should seek to know no more.

But he does look with a view to knowledge, to first causes, to the one image that will allow him to know what "it" is all about. He takes down the see-no-evil photograph, pins it in another place, and replaces it with the second blow-up of the fence that shows the hand holding the gun. The photographer is now in the center of the room, surrounded on three sides (left, front, and right) by photographs. The "action" in the park begins to unfold when the camera (for all intents and purposes along with the photographer) looks at the first enlargement of all (the girl pulling the man's arm). The basic serial arrangement of the photographs as the camera pans is as follows: (1) the girl pulling at the man's arm; (2) the distant shot of the embrace; (3) the blow-up of the embrace; (4) the blow-up where the man hides behind the fence; (5) the blow-up of the man holding the gun; (6) the enlargement of the girl and the man (the girl already breaking from the man's embrace and looking away, presumably having seen the photographer); (7) a two-part shot of the same photograph; the girl is well separated from the man, and the camera sees her first; then the camera sees the man by himself; (8) an extreme close-up of the girl looking away; (9) the see-no-evil photograph; (10) the distant image of the girl standing by the clump of bushes, forming an L-shape in conjunction with the torso of the dead man; (11) the distant image of the body by itself, after the girl disappears beyond the hill.[23]

As far as it is possible for the photographer to do, he has arranged his photographs so as to recreate the sequence of actions in the park. Yet there is no question but that the sequence itself, namely, the cinematic aspect of his discovery, does not in the least interest him. For out of the sequence he selects one image and makes it the dominant one, the one which of itself "explains" the action: "Ron? Something fantastic's happened. . . . Somebody was trying to kill somebody else. I saved his life." The image that he hangs on to, for now at least, is the blow-up of the hand holding the gun. Even if he sees the blow-up of the hand holding the gun in relation to other photographs he still makes it the central image, the clue. Certainly there ought to be no doubt that he has failed—just as he failed at the park—to see the images of the next-to-last photograph, the enlargement of the girl standing by the body. He thus narrates his findings, expressing the victory of photography, of analysis, and of the ego, over the dynamic, the organic, the colorful. He has invaded and subdued, so he believes, the cinematic world.

But of course his intellectual narrative is woefully incomplete. Aside from the fact that the photographic counterpart of the cinematic action of the park can never amount to a cinematic narrative because it was so abstracted in the first place, the photographer has failed to see the image of death—that is, the last image in the sequential arrangement in the studio. And in failing to see the image of death, he has yet to know it so that by knowing it he may somehow come to deny it. For the image of death is the image of his photographic self; it is the image that passes sentence on the visual crime that he perpetrates against the organic narrative energies.

Just as the photographer claims victory over the cinematic world, the cinematic world, in the form of the nymphs, triumphs over his photographic world. In this way the cinematic action proves in a concrete particular fashion that it has all along been narratively ahead of the photographer; that its departures from the photographer's point of view are no insignificant acts; and that it possesses a beneficent wisdom, manifested through its agents, the nymphs, that is painfully absent in the photographer.

But after the romp with the nymphs, the permanence he has ascribed to his ego is aligned with the most "permanent" of all the images in the sequence, namely, with the triply dead image. He doesn't hang on to this image of death because it is a fresh clue to a mystery. Rather, he hangs on to it—just after his inability to control the nymphs, the cinematic world incarnate—in a desperate effort to preserve and perpetuate his photographic self. In "dying" in a world of color, the photographer's first vision is that of the concomitant death of his substantial self as "photographer" as he comes to see it in the point of death occupied by the photograph of the dead body.

It is of little worth to rehash the narrative significance of the second blow-up session (the one that takes place after the nymphs leave). In many ways the same analytical inquiry takes place after they leave. But it is crucial to distinguish the two sessions in regard to the analytical endeavor of the second to deal with the image of the dead body. The cognitive yield of the analysis has only peripherally to do with the completion of the *story* whose existence the photographer has sensed from the time the girl comes to his studio-home for the pictures. The difference between the two blow-up sessions cuts much deeper, for initially the difference resides in the fact that in the second session the final blow-up, the white blotch, is totally segregated from every other image in the sequence. After the photographer returns from his second visit to the park, this becomes so

obvious as to be undeniable. All the photographs are gone except for
the final blow-up, which he finds between the two film storage
cabinets. Because the single image of death bears such a momentous
relation to the photographer, it is dangerous to assert categorically
that the other photographs have been "stolen" and to leave their
disappearance at that. The photographer has after all enacted a
process with the ultimate aim of discovering an end, a terminus, at
the expense of the process itself. It is accordingly fitting that in
seeking an end at the expense of the means, one image at the
expense of a sequence, an essence—indeed the very essence of
permanence—rather than an open-ended action, he and he alone
should be the victim of his own narrative mode. In his frantic but
futile search for the negatives and the 8 x 10s he looks for the way in
which he can reenact a sequence. Yet because he never really valued the narrative power of a sequence, and valued this sequence
only insofar as it could yield a single image, he would be reenacting
the process only so as to distill from it again the importance of one
image.

Then there is the importance that the photographer attaches to
the image of death so far as its very finality is concerned. For surely
the photographer has no real ethical stake in that image. (Later,
when Patricia asks him whether he should report the "murder" to
the police, the photographer doesn't even answer.) How, then,
does he come to be so obsessively attached to the image of death?
Recourse to a brief scene in the movie will help to explain.

The photographer pins the two blow-ups of "the body" directly
across from the wall in which the two blow-ups of the fence are
already pinned. He sits on the sofa, his back to the blow-ups of the
fence, looking at the blown-up images of death. Again, and for the
last time, he is the connection between the frozen images. From his
vantage point—aligned, that is, with the assassin—he in effect sees
himself as the killer.

Yet looking at the images of death he is also the killed. For he has
finished his second and final *completed* photographic act. He has
completed that act through the same abstractive, intellectual, and
analytical process in which his ego, his self-identity, his sense of
permanence, and his claim to visual supremacy are all bound up.
Like the session with the model, the photographic narration ends in
"death." But where "death" in the first complete photographic act is

affirmative and orgasmic (though certainly sterile), in the second it
is the terminus of photographic narration itself. The photographer's
encounter with the image of death is thus nothing less than his
encounter with the death of his own narrative mode. Because the
image of death has been blown up beyond recognition, the photographer cannot insist on the existence of a "real" counterpart of that
image, since anything in the public world that he would point to as
the white blotch's real counterpart would be "unlike" what the
white blotch shows. Moreover, photography and its attendant mode
of thought have been so far used to narrate a value *beyond* the
image: the image was a value only insofar as it generated a verbal
narrative, a statement—a statement on "the human condition," as
did the doss house photos or one about the "peace" and the "beautiful light" of the park, or an ethical statement, as when, through one
image, the photographer thought he had "saved somebody's life."
But now there is no narrative beyond the immediate encounter with
the image. It has become impossible *to name* it, *to infer* from it,
and, far more important, it has become impossible *to generate* other
images from it.

As the encounter with the triply dead image marks the death of
the photographic narrative mode, so does it by extension mark the
death of the photographer as a man the measure of whose life—as far
as he is concerned—is and can only be photographic narration. The
image of death narrates the photographer's own death as photographer. But this peculiar form of narrative reciprocity has no creative
consequences. So far as the relation between the narrating and the
narrated goes (and it is unclear which is which) no component in the
relation can exercise power over the possibilities of the other. No
doubt the image haunts the photographer. Yet beyond the sheer
persistence of its presence, the image can only make the photographer discover that the final manifestation of his search for knowledge about the image lies in the realization of the futility of just such
a search; he sees that his narrative passion is shot through with
negation; and, above all, he comes to grips with the unsettling
revelation regarding his conviction about the permanence and certainty of his own existence as a narrative creature.

The abstract image, though dead, has nonetheless performed a
creative feat, for it creatively negates those abstractions by which
the photographer has presumed to live. Permanence is death. Cer-

tainty is death. In a world of change—and what other world is there?—knowledge as an end in itself is the most obscene of luxuries. And death is the price the photographer as to pay for his criminal raid on the cinematic world, for his entrenched belief, no matter how unconscious, that the world of change is fair game for his egocentric pursuit of knowledge about images.

That the photographer dies to his narrative mode once he confronts the image of death in his own private world may mark the end of one phase in his dying process, but it does not make the death of the image a total evil—that is, it does not make the death of the image the final narrative "statement" of *Blowup*. If in his private world the photographer's concepts of permanence and certainty die, in his second visit to the park his notions of the "reality" he seeks in the image of the dead body die as well.

In the park once more, he wants to confirm the reality of the white blotch, of the indistinct final blow-up, in order to give it visual definition and thereby to ascribe to it an imperishable identity such as the one he believes he possesses. But a basic fact helps to underscore the futility of the photographer's involvement with the image of death: for once in the story he doesn't have his camera with him. For now, at least, photography is obsolete as an instrument for empirical verification. Photography cannot make public the private, egocentric reality which is, after all, what the photographer goes to see. Moreover, when he sees the dead man, when he encounters the "reality" he seeks, the dead man's eyes are open. Just like the photographer's, the dead man's eyes "look" but do not see. Because the photographer has no camera and because he looks directly at what looks back without seeing, there is revealed to him an even more disquieting intimacy with the image of death than that revealed to him in his private world. Hence the profound significance of not having his camera with him. The camera, the tool which is not an extension of his eye but of his ego, is not there to help him *prove* what his ego wants to see. He can't photograph the self. He can't photograph death. He can't photograph reality. He runs from the public world, all in a fright. His flight from the park clearly reveals his obstinate refusal to accept his own participation in the vision of a dead reality—which is to say in the vision of nothingness, since in a world of color in motion reality consists of the changes that moving color generates. He implicitly accepts the existence of the dead body. What he does not accept is his own visually unmediated relation to the image of the dead body.

What might well appear to be mere conjecture regarding the importance of the photographer's flight from the park once he encounters the image of death is clearly borne out in the scene in which Patricia comes to the photographer's after seeing him in her apartment while she and Bill were making love. Significantly, Patricia's first words are, "Were you looking for something just now?" She of course refers to the photographer's appearance in her apartment. But her words extend beyond such an immediate context, for in the park the photographer has been looking for the reality of the white blotch, and just moments earlier, after the disappearance of the photographs, he has been looking for the negatives and the 8 x 10s. Yet the photographer answers no to Patricia's question. His answer too extends beyond the immediate context of her question. It is, in fact, the first of several denials of the act of seeing in the scene. The rest of the pertinent dialog, illustrating the steady negation of seeing (and thus the photographer's attempt to disconnect himself from the image of the dead man), goes as follows:

The photographer: I saw a man killed this morning.
. . . .
Patricia: How did it happen?
The photographer: I don't know. I didn't see.
Patricia [quizzically]: You didn't see?
The photographer: No.

. . . .
The photographer [nodding toward the white blotch]: That's the body.
Patricia: It looks like one of Bill's paintings.

To say that this dialog fully explains itself because it suggests that the photographer's camera has seen something but that the photographer has not is an oversimplification.[24] For one thing, the photographer has seen what the camera saw. The enlargements earlier attested to that. But the rest of the photographs have disappeared. His initial narrative predicament in this scene accordingly amounts to having to narrate a visual action to Patricia without "visual aids." Therefore he begins by focusing the attention of his narrative (as he

has done so many times before) on a single image. Even if he has
only that single image left, the photographer's visual denial is clear
evidence of a process whereby what again becomes important is the
one image that allows him to draw a conclusion from a sequence of
visual events which is now in point of fact nowhere but in the ego.

The ultimate function of the narration of visual denial begins to
unfold with the photographer's distinction between himself and the
image of death. "That's the body," he says. "The body," like the
"leg" in Bill's painting, is a "that" outside the self. But while Bill
hangs on to that "that," the photographer—shocked as he has been
at the park to see that he is as dead as the man—seeks intellectually
to disavow any such intrinsic connection with the white blotch. If he
acknowledges his own connection with the white blotch he implicitly admits that he is as dead as "that" image, that the completion
of the photographic act marks the death of his ego, of his self-
identity. Thus the act of pointing at the white blotch, which is the
photographer's third interpretation of what he has seen at the park,
is intended to mean that permanence, certainty, and eminent reality are now dead as properties of the image. In this sense, he unwit-
tingly liberates the image that it may become a cinematic event. So
far, then, as his pronouncement of the death of the image's imperishable qualities goes, he announces the severing of the bond between himself and images. Even now, though he will take his camera to the park to "take a picture of the body," even now, though he
will retrieve his camera in the green expanse, the world is free from
the photographer's deadly narrative mode. And the concomitant to
the liberation of the image from photographic control is that there is
no longer a distinction between the actions that take place in the
private and in the public worlds. Shortly after Patricia goes out, the
photographer leaves his studio-home for good. The private world
disappears as one of the elements of narrative tension. There is no
longer a place where the cinematic world is in danger of becoming a
total abstraction. Insofar as the visual world ceases to exist for the
photographer's greater glory, narrative tension has in fact disappeared.

Yet through his intellectually motivated disclaimer of identity
with the "real" dead image ("the body") corresponding to the white
blotch, the photographer now attributes to himself all the qualities

(permanence, certainty, and eminent reality) that he denied to the final blow-up. He is the "this" outside the "that," the ego independent of the thing demonstrated.

But then "the body" is no body. It is "like one of Bill's paintings," abstract, ethereal, inhuman; and so it is, by extension, the image about which nothing can be known. Patricia will not corroborate the photographer's interpretation; she will not, this time figuratively speaking, massage his head (as she did literally, earlier in the story). And if there is no "that" neither is there a "this": an ego capable of intellectually pointing to an image whose "reality" derives from the ego's own concept of what should logically lie beyond the image. The photographer therefore needs another interpretive eye to confirm the permanence of his ego beyond the completion of a photographic act. What irony that the first witness should turn out to be Ron, Ron, who never listened! What even more profound irony that the final witness should be the still camera! For like the photographer's own eye, the camera never "saw."

The ego dies hard. The photographer takes to his camera again, his purpose being no more than to prove that he can see again, thereby to proclaim his changelessness and forge the world in the image of his "permanent" self. Thus the ultimate expression of the photographer's life lies in his pervasive belief that the world is as changeless as he wills himself to be. Such a fatal conviction about changelessness is especially revealed during the two blow-up sessions. But the photographer's faith in permanence is continually spilling over into images and events of that greater world, and it is in that world that such a belief is most clearly seen to be thoroughly ineffective.

The antique-shop owner, for instance, is as "fed up with antiques" as the photographer is "fed up with those bloody bitches." She is therefore selling the shop and going to Nepal. No sooner does the photographer sense her own narrative passion than he tells her, "Nepal is all antiques." He maliciously tries to discourage her from her adventure, almost as if sensing that because her zest for action is independent of his it can have no value. But she immediately says, "Perhaps I'd better try Morocco." She changes despite him. The photographer then sees the propeller and screams that he "can't live without it." He can't live without the part, the relation between the antique-shop owner and the photographer thus being a contrasting one: she can't live with the fragments of the past and must change; he can't live without them and must die with them.

It is no coincidence, then, that the antique-shop owner is never seen in relation to the fragmented images of the shop. She is surrounded by statues that are whole. In the right foreground there is a small statue of obviously African origin. Behind her, in the middle background, there is a whole statuette of a woman in neoclassical dress. The images that surround her are not only the images of wholeness, but the images of possibilities as well: if not Nepal, Morocco; if not the East, then Africa, or maybe even some other Western country. The images that surround her also show that her possibilities for change are boundless. And as if to accent further the irony of the photographer's cupidity, there is a photograph of a whole airplane to her back—one more indication that what the photographer settles for is a permanently fragmented existence in a world that is neither permanent nor fragmented.

Perhaps more important evidence undermining the photographer's conviction that he alone can generate change can be found among his last words to the girl as she leaves his studio: "Do I see you again?" In line with her wish to retain her invisibility, she doesn't reply. Then the photographer asks her for her name, her telephone number, trying to obtain a connection, no matter how abstract, whereby he may somehow see her again.

The photographer does see her again. But the visual act does not proceed from the "I." She just happens to be out on the street, standing under a sign (Permutit) which should alone tell the photographer that she has become the photographic image turned cinematic event.[25] She lives up to that sign when she disappears before his very eyes. The photographer tries to follow her, but to no avail. He gets hopelessly sidetracked, ending up first in a dark empty alley and then becoming one of the listless spectators of the Ricky Tick.

In contrast, the photographer no longer possesses the girl's "private" past. The girl's "permutation" proclaims her freedom from the control that the photographer had wanted to exert on her when he sought to transform her into one of his passive models. ("Have you ever done any modelling?" he asks. "Fashion stuff, I mean. You've got it." And pulling the lavender backdrop so she can pose in front of it, he tells her, "Hold that. Not many girls can stand as well as that.") The girl's disappearance also confirms the liberation of her photographic images from the photographer's private world. As they have vanished from the photographer's world, so does she vanish before his very eyes. In neither of the two disappearances is there a strict cause-and-effect relation. Both the photographic and the cinematic images change, and their transformations announce the disintegration of photographic narration as well as the pervasiveness of transitional energies as cinematic narrative powers.

But by far the most fatal, and yet the most beneficent, instance of the photographer's faith in the changelessness of his world is to be found in his assumption that "the body" is, as he says to Patricia, "still there." It is his most flagrant denial of a world of self-engendered change, and yet precisely because it is such a flagrant denial, it also constitutes the final phase of his photographic mode of narration.

Within his final movement toward death as an ego, the photographer goes through a process which, for the sake of clarity, can be divided into five phases: (1) his meeting with Ron at the party; (2) his discovery of the dead man's disappearance; (3) the scene with the mummers up to the moment when the photographer tosses the nothing ball back into the nothing court; (4) the "sound" of the nothing ball after the photographer tosses it back into the nothing court; and (5) his disappearance in the green expanse after he retrieves his camera. All the phases of this process, however, involve the photographer's presupposition that there is no change, that there will be, as he tells the nymphs, a photographic "tomorrow."

With all the urgency he can muster, the photographer says to Ron, "I want you to see the corpse. We've got to get a shot of it!" Ron, vacant, stoned, says, "I'm not a photographer." And the photographer angrily replies, "I am!" In a manner not unlike that in which Patricia demolished the photographer's interpretation of the white blotch and made him turn to Ron, Ron undermines the significance that the photographer ascribes to his vision of death and forces him to resort to the stupid, merely optical eye of his camera as the final witness. As a result, the photographer is already blind. When Ron asks him, "What did you see in that park?" the photographer replies, "Nothing." Thus because he asserts his existence in terms of his identity as photographer while at the same time claiming that he has seen "nothing," he denies his life as even the most rudimentary of visual creatures. "Nothing" is thus the fourth and final interpretation, if such it can now be called, of the photographer's encounter with the cinematic world.

At the park the photographer had said to the girl, "I'm a photographer." He could, or at least he believed he could, prove his existence in a formula such as *video ergo sum*. But now that photography is come to "nothing," there remains only the ego, adrift, pathetically yet presumptuously trying to prove its changelessness to itself. As the photographer's world itself changes, his narrative passion fails to develop. Narrative passion—the urge to change and to enact new relations to objects of change—is now a mere penchant for permanence, which is to say that it is actually no narrative passion at all.

Thus clinging fast to the last strand of photographic narration—which is now more properly transcendental narration—the photographer follows Ron into the den where the other living dead congregate. Once more (as when he tried to follow the blond man or the girl) he has gotten sidetracked. And once more he has fallen victim to his conviction that there is no change. Conviction thus acquires a double meaning. It is the belief that there is no change and it is the death sentence that the photographer passes on himself for so believing.

Then he awakens to "tomorrow," to a new day. He goes to the park, camera in hand, presumably to photograph "the body." But the body isn't there. Like the blond man, like the photographs, like the girl, it too has vanished without a trace, without a cause. It is at this point as accurate to say that the photographer has gone to see nothing as it is to say that he has gone to see the body. For since the photographer's assertion that he has seen nothing is so inseparable from the image of death, and since his ego is so bound up with the image of nothing, there is not a shred of difference between the disappearance of the body and the inexorable movement of the ego toward its own nothingness. In this way, both photography and its narrative consequences have had their one day, but cinematically there is no tomorrow for either. Thus there is no image of the self for the camera to see, and, as it turns out, the camera itself—with nothing to see—gives photographic narration its coup de grâce. Thus

for the photographer the intellectual consequences of the disappearance of the body come down to the fact that *intellectual* consequences are as such no longer possible. The photographer's belief in
the permanence that his ego can impose on the cinematic world dies
perforce when the body disappears. If he confirms something, it is
his own vulnerability to cinematic narrative energies. The consequences of the disappearance of the "real" image are cinematic—
imaginative, and not intellectual. For even that which is dead
changes.

But again, the ego dies hard. That no one visual reality can prove
the permanence of the ego in no wise alters the ego's consistent
effort to proclaim its own imperishableness, even when that imperishableness, totally insulated, is powerless to enact the most
elementary relation with the world. Hence the importance of the
encounter with the mummers and of the "sound" of the nothing
ball.

The mummers are a *class* of images, much in the same way as the
derelicts, the peace marchers, the "queers and poodles," the five
Africans, the audience at the Ricky Tick (except possibly for the man
and the woman who dance), and the living dead at the party, are all
classes of images the photographer encounters in the public world.
They lack individuality. Visually they have no particularity and are
therefore incapable of functioning creatively as discrete, individual
images. When the mummers first appear onscreen, their motion, as
a group (in the jeep), stops at the empty courtyard of a building
complex, which is in such a context a private world all its own. But
when in that same sequence they disperse and race away from the
empty courtyard, their actions have no direction. In the streets of
London they merely get lost among other classes of images, such as
the nuns, the royal guardsman (as a representative of a class), or the
derelicts themselves. Their only significant act early in the story is
visually to lead the camera in the direction of the photographer
when he comes out of the doss house, thereby contributing to the
creation of a contrast between themselves as a class of images and
the single image, the photographer's, who will shortly thereafter
slough off all connections with the derelicts with whom he has spent
the night.

Whenever the photographer comes into contact with any one

class of images, his impulse is to leave them behind for good. When, for instance, the mummers ask him for his money, he gives it to them and speeds away in his Rolls. He drives away from the peace marchers and even "sheds" their message. The Africans and the "queers and poodles" are never again seen. He leaves the audience of the Ricky Tick behind. And when he wakes up, all the living dead of the party have disappeared.

Only the mummers return. But just as their group motion in the streets of London is toward the deserted square of the building complex, so is their collective motion in the park directed toward the fenced-in and self-divided dark gray square within it, the tennis court. Abstractions themselves, they instinctively take to the abstraction within the natural world. By this time the tennis court is the single vestige of the photographic world.

The dumb show therefore finds its clear counterpart in that world of visual artifice that has for all intents and purposes ceased to function as the generator of narrative tension. In other words, the dumb show, with the "image" of abstraction (the nothing ball) as its central point of "visual " attention, is nothing but a recapitulation of the photographic mode of narration that has died with the disappearance of the body. The reality of the nothing ball parallels the intellectual activity whereby the photographer sought to ascribe a demonstrative reality to the image of death. And the nothing ball's "motion" across the court derives its reality from a purely conceptual act that forms the connection between the two halves of the court in a manner not unlike that in which the photographer's own ego was the "bedding" of his "sequence" of static images. Moreover, as the movie camera shows the limitations of photography during the blow-up sequence, so does it show the thoroughly photographic properties of the dumb show when it twice pans across the court, thus at once proclaiming the action an *abstr*action and clearly indicating that it, the movie camera, is an autonomous source of transitions even within such an inhibitive world.

The only significant difference between the nothing ball and the dead body, the photographer's visual activity and the mummers', the movie camera's action in the photographer's flat and at the tennis court, is that the reality of the mummers' game is derived from the collective consent of the mummers (the spectators as well as the players), whereas the demonstrative reality of the image of death issues from the photographer's isolated ego. In other words, as a class of images, as abstractions playing a game in an abstract world, the mummers can create a reality out of their dumb show—a reality which, as the camera clearly shows, is under no obligation to have its source in a visual event. The photographer is not as fortunate. He is, after all, alone. Even as he watches the dumb show he is well separated from the rest of the spectators. And yet for once claiming identification with a class of images, he eventually assents to the mummer's plea that he "retrieve" the nothing ball. But as the camera shows when it "follows" the nothing ball out of the tennis court and into the green expanse, the nothing ball loses its conceptual reality (as derived from the mummers' game) the instant it is outside the artificial world. And, as was stated above, losing its conceptual reality in the greenness of the natural world, the nothing ball also becomes less than nothing in that selfsame world.

With the passing of conceptual abstraction into the given world of cinematic action, the mummers themselves disappear. The camera never returns to the tennis court. Therefore any narrative affinities the photographer may have sought to establish with the mummers by retrieving the nothing ball also perish. But still, the nothing ball is his connection with a concept. In choosing to abide by the rules of the photographic even as he stands squarely in the cinematic world, the photographer in effect continues to insist on the integrity of his ego.

And ironically the act of relinquishing the nothing ball does not sever his connections with abstractions. The nothing ball is in this sense but one of the various fragments which, like the propeller or the guitar neck, the photographer gives up without at the same time giving up the belief in his own permanence. He may now be altogether blind, but he still hangs on to his conceptual being. So much so, in fact, that the new "reality" is sonic. The *sound* of the nothing ball is what becomes, for a brief instant at least, his new way of seeing, his way of demonstratively asserting his existence by proving to himself that he can retain the sense of his own permanence by ascribing sound to the nothing ball that he has just nothing-tossed back into a nothing-world. But it is worth remembering that the photographer has once before attempted to prove his existence sonically. Seeing himself alone on the street after failing to find the blond man, he honked the Rolls's horn in anger, in

frustration—as if in the absence of any image he had still to affirm
his own existence or be forced to admit, even at the height of his
ego's visual arrogance, that he had seen "nothing." Whether blow-
ing the Rolls's horn in the world of empty perspective or ascribing a sound to nothingness in a world that no longer exists, the ego
claims its supremacy, its eminence. In both cases the ego reveals its
antipathy to change.

So hard, then, does the photographer's ego die, that it cannot
even will itself to die. Even if it were to pronounce its own death,
the ego would continue perforce to adhere to that substantial, transcendental property by which it so strongly asserts its eminence.

But now the camera, which had been looking closely at the photographer as he "listened" to the sound of the nothing ball, suddenly looks at him in a long shot from a high angle, seeing him as a
"single point." In the luxuriant green, the photographer walks toward his still camera, which he had set down to retrieve the nothing
ball. He picks it up, and thus immediately shows his inability to
outgrow the photographic mode of narration, much less to embrace
a world of cinematic values. For, blind as he absolutely is, clutching
the stupid optical eye of the equally blind camera, standing motionless in the green expanse, and dressed in black and white, he is the
final photographic image. The movie camera cannot see his ego, but
it does see him as an image that so approximates the abstractions of
the conceptual self that there is no qualitative difference between
ego and image.

In this way, the photographer attains his devout wish to endure
as artifice in the organic world. In this way his return to his camera
implicitly proclaims what the movie camera does not, namely, that
"tomorrow," the new day, is as shot through with photographic
abstraction as yesterday, and that accordingly he is what he never
once has been, namely, the measure of the narrative. The photographer's very last image announces its readiness to raid the cinematic
world anew. And what is infinitely more perverse, it announces that
all the changes—the transitions and the transformations, the disappearances and the deaths, the births and the unexpected
creations—bear no ultimate narrative import. Denying change by
his very actions, he denies narration itself; he denies qualitative
relations; he denies life. In fine, he denies that anything new has

happened in the photographic yesterday and implicitly asserts that
nothing new will happen in the narrative today.

Unexpectedly, as unexpectedly as the nymphs invaded his private world, the photographer's image begins to fade from the green
expanse. It continues to fade until it altogether disappears. The
green expanse remains, showing beyond all doubt that the action,
from beginning to end, was primordially cinematic, and thus disclosing, conversely, that the photographer was all along the agent for
the celebration of the growth of cinematic values, for the celebration
of the life of qualitative transitions over which nothing else prevails
and which no amount of conceptual selfhood can control. Thus for all
its obstinate self-assertiveness, the ego dies a good death after all.
Because it happens in the cinematic world, the death of the ego
becomes a part of the festive occasion that *Blowup* opened with.

There are thus in *Blowup* two complete photographic acts—the
session with the model and the blow-up process leading to the triply
dead image. And there are also two whole cinematic acts, acts that
have their narrative origins in the given world. The photographic
acts are of themselves termini lacking creative consequences. The
cinematic acts are, on the other hand, both *termini a quo* and *termini ad quem*. They come to include the photographic acts, and thus
to qualify them; and in a very different sense, the two photographic
acts qualify the two complete cinematic acts by generating tension.
The first complete cinematic act, ending with the rape of the photographer by the nymphs, lays bare the futility of the photographer's
insistence on insulating himself from the liberating narrative energies of this world; it initiates the death-process of photographic
narration, and announces the possible birth of a new image of man.
The second cinematic act is the extension of the first, its "formal"
completion, and constitutes its own possibilities for the enactment
of a radically new narrative. (It reveals, like *Director's Notebook*, a
"perfectly incomplete" event.) It marks the photographer's final
dying, which is his consummation in the world. And it also marks
the satisfaction of the photographer's narrative passion in spite of
himself. It moreover marks the liberation of the world from an
archaic, a dominant, image of man, thereby making it even more
clear than at the end of the romp with the nymphs that a new image
of man can indeed emerge. And concomitantly, the completion of
the second cinematic act also signals the end of all intellectual as

well as visual perspective—it signals, that is, the wisdom of an
imagination that not only rebels against the image as a single point
(in the green expanse), but also announces its readiness to abandon
its own perspective *on* the image as the measure of its narrative
activity. The completion of the second cinematic act—which is more
accurately speaking a beginning—proclaims the advent of a new
narrative—a narrative in which the world's and man's image are, in
all their fabulous diversity, the unique sources of everything that
promises to carry forward discrete narrative acts to the vision of
those narrative tomorrows which are ultimately new ways of living
life.

4

Plasticity and Narrative Methods
THE CLOWNS

*The creativity of the world is the throbbing
emotion of the past hurling itself into a new
transcendent fact.*

ALFRED NORTH WHITEHEAD

At the very end of *Blowup* the entire screen is covered by the
green expanse of grass. The possibilities for a new narrative have
been fully announced, and the decks are clear to begin the excursion
into new cinematic values. The fact is, however, that the announcement of new narrative possibilities is as far as *Blowup* can go.
Such an achievement is in itself a major narrative breakthrough, for
Blowup reaches the threshold of a vision of man's new image in a
twofold sense: first, in relation to his contemporary cinematic existence; and second, in relation to his continually creative actions in a
world of qualitative transitions. But of itself *Blowup* can go no further. What it does it does at great expense. *Blowup* has expended
all its narrative energies in the disclosure of possibilities, and as a
consequence it cannot actualize a single one of those possibilities. It
can only lay them bare and thus offer them to imaginations bold
enough to begin where it leaves off. If the growth of cinematic
values is indeed one of the central events of contemporary life,
Blowup is among the handful of necessary movies. It is a
monumental cinematic departure from atavistic modes of narration.
Even if archaic modes of narration continue to attract attention,
Blowup is the living expression of the transition into new narrative
domains; it is the cinematic watershed that to this day makes of the
likes of *Seven Beauties* so much narrative old hat.
Accordingly, if *Seven Beauties* is the story of what might have

been and was not, *Blowup* is the story of what can be—and that not only in terms of movies to come, but also in terms of contemporary man's new vision of himself as a narrative creature in a world whose very essence is cinematic narration. In this respect too *Blowup* is one of the most important movies of the postwar era (perhaps one of the most important movies ever). For its fundamental genius lies in its clear vision of an image of man—of a man to be—who can no longer continue to resist the narrative energies that create his life, who can no longer continue to ignore the new creative powers that are the vehicles for his adventure into new moral and esthetic terrain. *Blowup* thus attests to the fact that man cannot continue to proclaim himself the measure of all things; that he cannot insist on searching for an enduring substance; that he cannot continue to engage in a quest for certainty; that he had better abandon his penchant for mastery over the creation; that he must desist from endeavoring to turn this world into a paltry metaphor for reductive convictions, born of overintellectualizations, which tell him there is a better world than this; that he had best relinquish his hold on that dear, precious, and cowardly egocentric aloofness that allows him to contemplate, now cynically, now despairingly, his own vicissitudes in this perpetually perishing world of creative change. Man is an image of his own and the world's continual creation. His salvation is either in this world or it is nowhere at all.

Thus where *Seven Beauties* was a clear summons to a continued critical inquiry into other narrative alternatives if only because it rendered an unsatisfactory vision of man's contemporary image, *Blowup* is the rallying call to narrative action in the world itself. To be humanistically complacent with a mere "appreciation," or even worse, with an "understanding" of *Blowup*'s feat is to miss its narrative significance altogether. It is part and parcel of *Blowup*'s narrative importance that it looks prospectively beyond it for a new image of man.

For it is indeed the absence of an active image of man that prevents *Blowup* itself from actualizing the narrative possibilities that lie beyond the threshold it reaches. *Blowup* lacks a concrete, particular narrative agent, an agent who will slough off his burdensome intellectualism, will cross the threshold unafraid, explore, and in fact *become* what lies beyond. This is to say that the precise manner in which *Blowup* expends its narrative energies in unfolding the possibilities for new narrative realms is through the examination of contrasting narrative modes which are forever engaged in dubious battle in the same visual plain. It is in just such a battle of contrasts that the narrative import of *Blowup* comes to be felt as a landmark event. *Blowup* is then not only the story of what can be; it is also, at least by implication, the story of what can no longer be a living value, not so much in terms of other movies—*Seven Beauties* is after all one of many enticing movies since the time of *Blowup*— but in terms of thought about the movies.

Still, for all the creative function of the nymphs and for all the presiding imagination's own capacities to show value in the transitory nature of life in both the public and the private worlds, *Blowup* is saddled with the image of the photographer as its sole human "protagonist." The other protagonist is the camera, the presiding imagination, the most consistently creative function of which is to narrate as life itself narrates. The photographer, on the contrary, lives against the imaginative beat, against the cinematic pulses and impulses of the given world. Accordingly, he perennially divorces himself from whatever possibilities his narrative passion may bear. His actions, in a word, never wholly coalesce with the world's. He sunders his own life from the greater events about him— from the fabulous, from the unexpected, from the adventurous.

He is a photographer, in substance, in being. And he lives the life of his photographic being—along with its welter of human consequences—to the very hilt. Today is photographic, and so is tomorrow and tomorrow. And in the meantime, in the absence of a human image such as might consistently show that the photographer is more properly the *an*tagonist, the presiding imagination must singlehandedly continue to undermine the existence of a photographic tomorrow. The imagination will here and there no doubt introduce discrete images as foils to the photographer's ego—images such as the nymphs, the antique-shop owner, and, even to a certain extent, the girl herself. But the imagination (as the movie camera) also bears the brunt of creating narrative tension; and to it as well falls the even more difficult task of resolving that tension. No discrete human image energized with the narrative élan of the camera ever emerges from within *Blowup*'s cinematic tomorrow. So the camera has to end its activity by proclaiming that though the given world be ever so ready for a new individual, the new individual is not ready for the given world.

As a result, what perhaps best defines the image of man in *Blowup* is "character"—that is, etymologically speaking he is a being with an indelible mark. This being, ever present in the photographer's image, finds its most fundamental expression in terms of a permanent self-identity in relation to the changing world.[1] His character flaws his narrative passion. His character, that is to say, wants change, but it wills to remain a character all the more. Conversely—and what is more appropriate for the purposes of the present chapter—the photographer's narrative passion lacks plasticity, or the readiness to change in concert with the changes that the world generates all along. The photographer—more ego than image—is a character without the faintest trace of plasticity. No matter how alienated he is from all the classes of images with which he ever comes into contact, he clings to his identity. (Perhaps because he is the only photographer in the story, exclusive of course of the one in the credit sequence, the photographer is more jealous of his identity as such. But even such an identity as this is a far different thing from individuality.) The best, then, that can be said of man's image in *Blowup* is that it loses its identity, its character, without ever stepping across the threshold and into individuality.[2] The photographer disappears from the world, and inasmuch as he does so he loses his identity. *But the price of losing his identity is the loss of his image.* Thus whatever possibilities for individual narrative action may inhere in his image are irretrievably lost along with his identity—whether as photographer or as transcendental ego. Therefore, in this respect also, *Blowup* reaches the threshold: it announces the plastic qualities of the new narrative man in an equally plastic world, but it stops short of locating specific methods whereby the life of the plastic individual image can grow to be a value. It is in the discovery of such methods for creating the image of a new man that *The Clowns* can be seen as successfully crossing the threshold of those new narrative possibilities which *Blowup* only points to.

That in *The Clowns* the image of man has developed into a much more sophisticated phenomenon than it is in *Blowup* is immediately

borne out by the disarmingly simple fact that the "central image,"
Fellini himself, is a moviemaker.[3] The cinematic is therefore the
presupposed mode of narration from beginning to end.

Indeed, not only in contrast to *Blowup*, but in comparison with
Director's Notebook itself, *The Clowns* makes a narrative advance
all its own. Where *Director's Notebook* begins with the images of
ruins and with a Fellini who, among the ruins, merely laments the
past, *The Clowns* begins with a young Fellini whose passion is
immediately to participate in a visual adventure. Accordingly, the
narrative tensions that arise in the course of *The Clowns* are conflicts regarding the discovery of the most illuminating, of the most
humanly significant, cinematic narrative mode. That is, in *The
Clowns* narrative tension is not manifested in terms of two radically
opposed and utterly irreconcilable ways of seeing the world. *The
Clowns* is rather a process of matching a narrative method to an
underlying narrative passion. This movie exemplifies a direct, indeed almost a relentless, way of going at the heart of the satisfaction
of an underlying narrative craving. In this respect, *The Clowns* not
only represents an advance beyond *Blowup*, but also beyond the
structural hopscotch of *Director's Notebook*, which for all its genius,
lacks the directness of *The Clowns*.

At any rate, from the beginning, Fellini is out to make a movie.
Thus the image of man in *The Clowns* is the cinematic imagination
incarnate. This is not to say, however, that Fellini's narrative passion is from the outset in perfect harmony with the world in which
he seeks to make his movie. If such were the case, there would be
no narrative, no discovery, no change, no growth of cinematic and
humanistic values. And conversely, the narrative passion itself could
not exist without a vague yet insistent craving for narrative adventure. So far, in fact, is *The Clowns* from being throughout a mere
consequence of Fellini's initial narrative predispositions that it is in
many respects the narration of a story that makes itself in spite of
Fellini. Therefore insofar as Fellini wants to impose his directorial
control over his "subject-matter"; insofar as throughout a great portion of the story he considers himself to be the measure of all things
visual; and insofar as he believes that his world cannot creatively
transform him, he has a great deal in common with the photographer. Indeed, Fellini vanishes from *The Clowns*, as the photographer does from *Blowup*. But in *Blowup* the disappearance of the

human image marks the end of man's participation in the cinematic world, while in *The Clowns* the disappearance of the "central image" is no less momentous an affair than the disappearance of one man as the force that pretentiously seeks to control the narrative passions of the world itself.

From this general observation about *The Clowns* a second one issues: in *The Clowns* the world itself and all the variety of images that act within it become particularized, individualized, precisely because there is no ultimate world and no final, archetypal image of man. The world itself is particularized as an event, as an action. This eventful world is the circus ring, about which much more will have to be said in this chapter. The individualized images are, generally speaking, the clowns and the other performers in the circus ring. A great deal remains to be said about them, too. For now, however, it is important to state that the clowns are not a class of images, that they are not visually indistinct abstractions expressive of what is at most a vague and generic activity. (If Fellini has a tendency to think of the clowns as such, that's his problem, and it is a problem that he grows to solve imaginatively.) Let there be no mistake about it: the clowns bear none of those identifiable and classifiable characteristics that are so much present in the images of the bohemians in *Director's Notebook* or of the mass men or the prostitutes in *Seven Beauties* or of the mummers, the peace marchers, and the models in *Blowup*. Not only are the clowns not a class of images, but they also have the capacity to enact a process of individuation all their own (much as the hopefuls in *Director's Notebook* do). They narrate their own stories. Or, more accurately, they enact narrative energies that allow them to become, each one in his own way, sources for the fulfillment of Fellini's narrative passion. They therefore become so many "central images"; and for this reason they not only liberate Fellini's own imagination from having to control them, but also, and what is immeasurably more important, they make the profoundest mockery of the traditional distinctions between art and life. Each is a chief image in his own moment. Each contributes in his own specific way to the narration of joy. Each is a link between art and life.

But even when the action of *The Clowns* does not take place inside the ring, the world is a ring—so long as Fellini lets it be; it is a center of narrative action with none of those onerous intellectual abstractions found in the square, segregated, and self-divided private world of the tennis court in *Blowup*. And even when the participants are not professional clowns, they narrate—sometimes against Fellini's will—the laughter and the joy that Fellini himself gropes for, first intellectually (or historically), and later artificially (by presenting a narrative action within the ring—Fischietto's funeral—which only appears to be spontaneous, organic, and autonomous when in fact Fellini has been controlling it all along). Art and life eventually become inseparable. The unity of art and life—which is the ultimate gift to men—is the keynote of *The Clowns*.

The first event narrated in *The Clowns* is not visual. While a red screen behind the movie's title prevents any particular image from being revealed, a voice of command is heard over music. Then the red screen disappears and the image of a boy in bed emerges. Awakened by the voice, the boy gets up, turns on the light above his bed, draws the curtains, opens the window, and looks at the circus tent as it is raised. He runs to his mother to announce what he has seen: "The circus is here." Next morning he is out of the house, looking up at the tent, ignoring the elephant as well as the midget who hoses it. The boy is next inside the tent, looking at the empty ring. Then, assuming the boy's own relation to the ring, the camera moves toward its center. A short man in top hat, coattails, and riding boots enters the ring from the opposite end. He then looks at the camera, winks his eye, flashes a good-natured smile at it, and turns around to the show ponies, which now run in circles inside the ring.

Basically, what has occurred in this initial sequence—from the voice over the title to the motion of the boy/camera toward the ring—is a movement toward the center (the circus ring), which is to become the location for almost every positive narrative occasion in the story. More than an arbitrary ploy to introduce the movie, this sequence functions to provide an organic model for the growth of the narrative action. The voice of command is heard time and again in the person of Fellini as both participant and verbal narrator in the story. It is the voice of the man in his search for a "lost" joy. The voice also appears later on, during the funeral sequence; it is the voice of Fellini as director, as the man who, surreptitiously as it were, manipulates and controls the images and their actions. Moreover, the relation of the child to the tent and to the ring itself parallels the conditions of Fellini's various *personae* throughout the action. As the child is initially outside the tent, so is Fellini, as both participant and verbal narrator, prevented from an immediate connection with the object of his search. As both the child and the camera subsequently make their way into the tent but see only the empty ring, so Fellini, the director presiding over Fischietto's funeral, moves outside the inhibitive confines of the past as a source for narrative passion at the same time that he remains as incapable as ever of enacting a union with the miraculous outbreak of color at the culmination of the funeral sequence. And the moment when the child/camera moves to the center of the ring and sees the trainer and his ponies is a vivid prelude to the instant, shortly following the funeral sequence, when the "director's" subjective narrative fiat, his point of view, vanishes and is replaced by the story of the old clown, which itself fulfills the narrative aspirations of Fellini's *personae* and releases the story of the quest for joy from the onus of the historical and the artificial forms of narration, freeing it for the vast potentialities for unity available in the pluralistic world of visual relations without a controlling intellectual perspective.

As a direct result of its structural affinity with the events of the first sequence, *The Clowns* vividly displays the pursuit and subsequent discovery of joy, and particularly joy in and through the visible creation. The search is initially propelled by a sense of lost innocence articulated by the mature Fellini as a participant in the story. As he dictates to Maya, his secretary, Fellini bemoans the loss of the "exhilaration" that was once his. Yet the outcome of *The Clowns* attests to the movie's having abandoned Fellini's initial wish merely to recapture the joys of childhood images. Indeed, since the scene in which Fellini yearns for the past as he dictates to Maya follows immediately the sequences of the circus and of the village folk as seen by the child, it is clear that the images that frightened the child are now "idealized" by the maudlin, sentimental spirit of the mature man. Evidently the lost "exhilaration" can be attained only through a radical divorce from the immediacy of the visual experience. It can be enacted only through the imposition of a fixed point of view—of an intellectual perspective not unlike the photographer's—on a world that has already been denied its own visual expressiveness if only as a result of being imported into the realm of Fellini's memories. The narrative passion that launches the quest is shot through with an abstract sentimentality that can have no foundation in the actual past, because the child was terrified by the images in the ring. With nothing but sentiment to create from, the mature man cannot transform visual fear into visual delight. Yet a persistent zest for narration is also present in the initial encounter with the mature Fellini. Such a pervasive urge comes to manifest itself as the power for action whose fundamental direction depends on the quality of its interaction with images. Thus "exhilaration" is not only the ironic expression of an irredeemable "fall" from an innocent condition; eventually it is the narrative passion itself, actualizing the potentialities of images, not as abstractions but as presentational events, and making of the story not a remembrance of things past but a unified sequence of changes with a specific source of satisfaction located in the contemporary world. Accordingly, what was in the previous chapter referred to exclusively as *narrative passion* in order to signify the urge for creative change will in this chapter be assigned the more inclusive term *esthetic aim*. Fellini himself, by the use of the word *exhilaration* suggests that both the narrative passion and its objects are of an intrinsically esthetic nature; that the change he desires to narrate himself into is not intellectually but ineffably joyous. At the same time, *esthetic aim* is a phrase that goes far beyond the paltry romantic rhetoric that absorbs Fellini early in the story. The phrase articulates and incorporates the transitions made in and by the story, primarily through visual events, on behalf of the final vision of joy. Also, the terms *passion, craving, yearning, impulse, urge, zest,* and *adventure,* with appropriate modifiers, are used as more specific substitutes for esthetic aim. Of course, this does not mean that narrative passion ceases to operate as the underlying activity throughout *The Clowns.* The expansion of the term narrative passion is dictated by the action itself, an action whose narrative thrust is aimed at the discovery of joy, of entertainment, of the freedom of the human spirit in the world of free images.

From the moment the boy awakens to seek visual adventure beyond the safety of his home, *The Clowns* illustrates the persistent search of the creative urge for self-clarification and for eventual unification with its ideal object of satisfaction. In the last scene, when the two clowns unite, leave the ring, and disappear in the spotlight, it is evident not only that the esthetic impulse has discovered the integration of past, present, and future, but also that it has reconciled innocence with the present, the imagination with the intellect and with memory, and the visual powers with the verbal. But the development of such a story does not depend on creative zest alone. The esthetic aim requires a method (or methods) to carry it to its fulfillment. Therefore in addition to being the story of a search for joy, *The Clowns* is also the story of the modes of narration capable of satisfying the underlying aim. *The Clowns* is not only the story of the "what," but also of the "how."

Since these narrative modes delineate specific substructures within the story, it is impossible to examine them in isolation from the events themselves or even apart from the narrative commitment whence they spring. But it is vital to keep sight of the fact that these modes of narration pass into subsequent ones and are of themselves wholly functional: they are not only instruments for the manifestation of the sought joy, but, so far as they are individually able to be, they are also embodiments of the progress of the story toward its joyous vision. This means that the first two narrative methods are not mere tricks to demonstrate their own ineffectiveness in contrast to the method that finally carries the enduring passion to its satisfaction. Rather each method is part of a process; it is in itself an "extensive" sequence of narrative visions. To slur over them in order to deal the more directly with the mode whereby the sought joy is attained would amount to a gross disregard for the continual unfolding of narrative values, of values which ultimately reside as much in the narrative process as in any "final" vision.

The narrative modes, then, are plastic. They metamorphose into each other, helping to shape the matrix for organic action. And thus, by extension, so is the esthetic aim itself plastic: ever undergoing, no matter how reluctantly at times, new transitions—changing every time a specific mode of narration fails to satisfy it. As the narrative methods adapt to the esthetic aim, so does the aim adapt to the methods the instant that the aim senses that a method has reached its narrative limit.

The first of the three narrative modes is historical narration. Since it relies on the verbal predispositions of Fellini as the principal participant in the first part of the story, the action is ineluctably connected to Fellini's intellectually biased inquiries about an idealized past. All through this part, "narrative" functions in its most orthodox sense, that is, as a tale told in words, to which the moving image is for all intents and purposes mere embellishment. Fellini *tells* of his "exhilaration"; he tells who his collaborators are; he tells where he is, where he goes, and to whom he goes in order to receive equally intellectual responses to his questions about clowns. The historical mode, then, begins with the voice of command over the title and ends with the voice of Fellini asserting that perhaps Tristan Rémy, the circus historian, "is right, maybe the clown really is dead."

Immediately following Fellini's verbal assertion—which in effect amounts to a momentary interruption of the pervasive zest—Fischietto's funeral, and thus the second narrative method, begins. It "begins" as little more than the visual form of "the clown's" death as pronounced by the historical narration. But by the end of the second narrative mode, the elegy on "the clown" is transformed to a vision of resurrection into a world of color. Yet from outside the ring the voice of Fellini, the "director," says, "Turn it off. It's over." The disembodied voice reemerges as a narrative force imposing itself upon the possibilities for the satisfaction of the enduring aim.

The voice, a dominant force during the historical narration, is absent during the second narrative mode, however. It reemerges only to end the funeral sequence. In fact, the reliance on cause-and-effect relationships, so characteristic of the historical narration, is for all practical purposes absent from the funeral sequence. The energies for satisfaction reside in the action in the ring. Having disappeared as a character, as an ego saturated with self-identity and with the will to know about the past, the "I" which tells has been replaced by the eye. Yet it is just as evident that this potentially creative eye remains outside the ring. Early in the funeral sequence Fellini stands by the camera dolly, his eye to the viewfinder, and walks backward away from the center of the ring. His opportunity to explore and develop the initial relationship between the child, the camera, and the center of the action is repressed in favor of an egocentric disdain for the active center, and such a disdain in turn allows him, he believes, to preside over the direction of the activity in the ring while of course pretending that he does not.

The only other time the "director" is seen in this sequence—and for that matter in the rest of the movie—he is a spectator sitting outside the ring. He talks to an intellectual interviewer and tries to reduce the action in the ring, as well as his own narrative craving, to a "message." As a result of his total failure to participate in Fischietto's rebirth, the subjective "director" seeks control of the action and declares its end in a manner not unlike the one in which he declared the barrenness of the world of clowning at the end of the historical narration. The second narrative mode, then, is artificial. In it, the relation-making power has as its fundamental assumptions the notions that both change and motion are illusory and that growth and freedom are inconsequential accidents to a thinking substance. Accordingly, all that is new and all that is possible in the new is turned into artifice by the presiding consciousness; it is staged, as it were, by an ego masquerading as an eye which will do naught but photograph, direct, and edit the energies of images.

During the third narrative mode the voice of the old clown is never divisive.[4] Instead it is the opening phase of a process leading to the actualization of the passion to see and create joy. The clown's story of death and rebirth triggers the third and final narrative mode. Eventually shifting the source of narration from Fellini's mediating *personae* to the individual participants in the action within the ring, the clown's verbal account transforms the relation-making pattern of the story from a subject-object dualism to an interaction between the aim—now expressed by the clown—and its possibilities for actualization in the organic present. The immediate result is the liberation of the action from the controlling, "directorial" forces that preside throughout the two preceding narrative modes. Since the clown, once the "object" of Fellini's ego, enacts the new narrative, the disintegration of Fellini's narrative by dualism allows the action to go beyond the passive connection between the child/camera and the pony trainer in the center of the ring. The attenuation of dominant, restrictive subjectivism, of intellectual point of view, is replaced by a sudden revelation, development, and clarification of imaginative powers heretofore existing as half-realized or merely verbalized expressions of the underlying zest evoked throughout the two previous patterns of narration by the mature Fellini. In short, the esthetic aim, seemingly Fellini's

private domain, is suddenly manifested in the very object of his
search, that is, in the old clown who, like Fellini himself, searches
for the life of joy.

The old clown's story signals the final motion toward unity by
enacting the inherent relatedness of the past to the present and of
the aim to the creative powers of the individual. The third mode is
genial in an etymological sense: that which clearly emerges from the
little old clown's approach to the creative impulse is the spirit of
generation and birth. The genial narration is itself clearly composed
of three phases. In the first, the little old clown *tells* the story of his
old act. In the second, the first clown who plays the trumpet appears
miraculously at the far end of the stands. But then the eye of the
camera follows the spotlight that discovers the second clown at the
other end of the stands. This visual initiative toward uniting the two
clowns is the third phase of the genial mode.

Before Fellini's voice appears as the force that generates the
historical narration, the camera, an extension of the child's passion
to see, goes on its first tour of the attractions within the ring.[5] It sees
the feat of strength performed by Robor, the masked strong man,
when he stands under the immense, bullet-shaped weight. Immediately, the camera witnesses the energy and the strength of the
image as well as its capacity to endure a burden imposed upon it.
Following the strong-man act, however, the camera sees a parody of
Robor's feat performed by a midget who does not wear a mask. Thus
the camera also announces the capacity of images to display their
energies fully and to turn them into laughter and into freedom from
extraneous burdens. The camera then sees the knife-throwing performance, and a midget comes close to the camera with an expression of mock horror and a scream every time a knife is thrown at the
woman. The midget serves as both participant (acting within the
ring) and audience (as a result of his horrified expressions). It is
clear from this early event that the divisive considerations that
plague Fellini as both participant and "director" when he attempts
to make a story from the actions in the ring are never present in the
ring itself.

After these events, still in the same relation to the ring, the
camera sees Matilde fight and easily defeat the champion wrestler, a
man who, in a world which does not promote social norms or foster

conventional ethics, has, as a male, no more power than does the woman. And when the ringmaster offers prize money to any spectator who will accept Matilde's challenge, one of them, immediately dubbed Miss Tarzan by the ringmaster, steps into the circle to fight her. As a midget in a previous act is not seen cooked and devoured, so the fight between Matilde and Miss Tarzan remains unseen. The significance of the event resides in the fact that an image from the outside enters the ring in order to participate in the action. There is no intellectually definable "bedding" that mediates the transitions between the inside and the outside. The ring includes itself, the world outside, and the unmediated, self-generated transitions between the two. The confrontation between the two amazons is contrasted with the next act, where Fakir Burmah goes underground, as the ringmaster says, "forty days and forty nights, without food or water." The mystic, the transcendental man who interacts with no image, who is motionless and who does not nourish his body, steps into a coffin, is covered with a blanket, and buried, never to be seen again. The action in the ring, even at such an early stage, clearly shows that death befalls him who conceptually deems himself above narration, above relations.

Then the ringmaster introduces the boy/camera to Neptunia and to Adriano, her attendant midget, who is in love with her. Neptunia's "cold-bloodedness," her pale complexion hidden by the flamboyant dark glasses, and her appetite for goldfish do not deter Adriano from attempting to win her love. Adriano is in love with an image, individual and unique, not with a woman in whom he seeks traditional attributes of beauty.

In the final scene of this sequence, the ringmaster brings into the ring the fish tank containing the fetuses of the Siamese twins. They are, he says to the audience, "united in life and in death." Then, moving toward the camera at the edge of the ring and looking straight at it (thus explicitly singling out the individual), he asks, "You see them, little boy? Aren't they nice?" The innocent eye of the boy is challenged to see from an unmediated center of visual action. He is not challenged to see just the Siamese twins. Indeed, the boy is asked to see joy in all the images that have so innocently displayed their beneficent powers before him during the entire sequence. He is asked to behold the images' vitality, to participate in and to witness their immanent creativity, to witness their continual readiness to assimilate and beget changes, their capacity to excite love, their ability to lead the eye beyond rational concepts of reality and illusion, truth and falsity, good and evil, or beauty and ugliness, their energy to transcend logic, intellectual categories, and notions of substance. In short, the boy is asked to embrace the vast diversity of visual narrative powers that can lead his eye into a celebration of those very powers.

Then, almost instantly after the questions are posed to the boy by the ringmaster, trumpets sound and numerous clowns rush into the ring. Throughout this outbreak of actions, one clown, the thin one with the tall top hat sways silently, smilingly over the edge of the ring, uniting the outside with the inside. At the edge of the ring, two clowns hit each other over the head with the ever-growing hammer which one of them takes away from a third clown who tries to drive a huge nail into the wooden edge of the ring while a spectator holds the nail for him. When the third clown finally gets to swing his huge sledgehammer, he misses the nail and instead hits the spectator on the head. Again the action in the ring bursts from within its confines. Up close to the camera and right in front of it, another clown fires a cannon, and the bullet, protruding from another's rear end, fires back in the direction of the cannon. Then the cow, terrifying to the other clowns, rushes into the ring and in the direction of the camera, comes to an abrupt halt, turns, runs to a chair in the center of the ring, sits down, crosses its legs, and drinks wine from a bottle. Thus enabled to enact a narrative of unity all its own, the action in the ring proclaims that it is the cinematic world incarnate, that it is the power whose value Fellini must grow to embrace. The action can do without Fellini as "master director." There is no indispensable consciousness. The only requirement is a festive eye capable of imagining (and thus of celebrating) the actions in the ring.

The antics of these clowns are distinguished from the previous events in the ring not only by the formal announcement made by the trumpets, but by the fact that, unlike the feats performed by Robor or Matilde and unlike the images of Fakir Burmah or Neptunia, all these events take place either just inside the ring or are directly aimed at the child/camera. All the actions of the clowns are for the delight of the individual who has been invited to see by the ringmaster. As a result, the first sequence with the clowns provides ample evidence that the center of vision remains to be developed and qualified into a narrative force capable of accepting the gift of images as a precondition of the satisfaction of the enduring aim.

But suddenly the boy, his back in the foreground throughout all of these events, is taken away from his seat at the edge of the ring by his mother. He is crying in fear. His return to his room shows that he is incapable of visual assent to the ringmaster's questions about the Siamese twins. His adventure into the circular, organic world of visual action is abandoned for the safety of the familiar, rectangular frame of the window by which he now stands, staring into the darkness, seeing nothing. The zest for visual novelty is blurred by tears.

It is at this moment that Fellini's voice-over emerges and recapitulates what has just taken place, saying that the clowns did not make him laugh. "No," this disembodied voice says, "they frightened me," and it goes on to tell of the "chalky faces," the "enigmatic expressions," "the twisted, drunken masks and the absurd, atrocious jokes" of the clowns as the objects of horror. The first words of the mature voice articulate the boy's own visual abnegation. The voice continues: "They [the clowns] reminded me of other strange and troubled characters who roam around every country village."[6] The voice avails itself of memory as a distancing device. Along with analysis, memory becomes a major component of the historical narration. From its first appearance as a narrative vehicle until its final disappearance, memory isolates the narrator from the fulfillment of the esthetic aim by turning him away from the process of convergence with the center of action which was immediately accessible to the boy.

It is obvious that the events in the ring, from Robor's performance to the antics of the clowns, are of a fantastic nature. Not a single one of these actions lies in the past experiences of the boy. Since he is unable to recognize their narrative energies, the boy's perceptual world, previously limited to the environment of the home, is creatively destroyed by them. Inevitably, therefore, the questions posed to the boy—not only "do you see them?" but also "aren't they nice?"—find their way into his life in terms of an implicit demand either that he embrace the abundance of forms and of narrative possibilities in the visual world or that he reject them altogether as ludicrous and incongruous with what is possible. Fellini's voice asserts that, like Big John, the midget nun, the town drunk and his wife, the mutilated war veteran and his single "shock troop," Signora Ines, the stationmaster, the Fascist official, and Giudizio, the clowns too are gross anomalies of the visible creation; that they are visually inconsistent with the norm of limited visual experiences to which the boy was accustomed or in which the mature man himself, Fellini, seeks to discover his "exhilaration."

For this reason, then, the "flashback" to Fellini's hometown entails an implicit narrative perversity. Its main purpose is to show the "grotesqueness" of human images. Fellini imposes his own readymade sense of visual order, of visual harmony, symmetry, and proportion on a variety of visual experience that does not submit to such an imposition.[7] Only his pure intellectual being can consider "chaotic" and "troubled" that which is inconsistent with his equally pure intellectual notions of what the object of his narrative passion ought to be. If there were no intellect to classify and categorize, then Fellini might come to see that strangeness itself is a fundamental value. For strangeness is after all no more than the perception of discreteness in diversity, of uniqueness in multiplicity; it is the incipient vision of the narrative powers of the individual.

But because Fellini does intellectualize the human images of his hometown, the strangeness of the individual "characters" (which are in point of fact images), disturbs him. And what is more pathetic still for Fellini himself, the uniqueness of these images will not let him laugh with them. On the contrary, if anything, he implicitly laughs *at* them. In all his intellectual aloofness, he cannot participate in that world save as a disembodied voice which, in feeling mere sympathy for the "grotesque" images, in effect asserts its superiority over them. Laughter, in a word, is never on the verge of passing into joy.[8]

Conversely, in the same "flashback" to the child's hometown, the insipid, lyrical scene with the equally insipid blonde in the poolroom clearly "fascinates" Fellini ("Fascination" plays in the soundtrack from the moment of the blonde's entrance). The blonde is Fellini's archetypal image of woman; she is an empty, symbolic throwback to his obsession with ideal images of women in several of his previous black-and-white movies.[9] No sooner does the blonde enter the poolroom than she becomes the object of visual adoration for all the *vitelloni*. In this way, both the fascination of Roy, the

cameraman, with Liana Orfei and that of Fellini and his crew with
Anita Ekberg complement this fascination of Fellini's with an archetypal image, with an image that the eye feels *familiar* with, and
able only to contemplate passively as the embodiment of so many
intellectually endearing abstractions.[10] And yet it takes Giudizio—to
Fellini's intellect the most pathethic of these "characters," but
actually the most "genial" of the village folk—to deflate the blonde's
archetypal beauty when he says that if the blonde gives him five lire
she may have sexual intercourse with him. The *vitelloni* laugh with
"poor" Giudizio. And even after they have their mock war with the
patriotic Giudizio (who goes into his martial fits only after he sees
war movies), they call a truce, as it were, and join with him in
laughter.[11]

At this time Fellini's voice-over ironically affirms that the mature
man is as inept a visual creature as the boy was. Clearly the man is
unable to assimilate all he sees (or at least most of what he remembers seeing) as a way of getting on with the task of living in, growing
with, and creating from a world of images. But despite the voice's
maliciousness, this first explicit instance of the historical mode of
narration succeeds in hinting at a vital connection between art and
life. Accordingly, while the historical method is of itself doomed to
call attention to art's divorce from life by alienating the known past
from present possibilities, the voice cannot help but show the organic relation between the clowns and the townspeople and between the circus ring and the visual creation. That is, when the
voice attempts to illustrate the "grotesqueness" of the clowns it does
so from images encountered in life itself. Despite Fellini, the action
links life, the art of clowning, and the making of a movie.

It is also significant that Alvaro, the sound-man, is the sum of the
mutilated war veteran's "shock troops," and that Gasperino, the
"head grip," is one of the coachmen who playfully break wind outside the railway station. These men who will soon appear in the
story as members of Fellini's film crew are present among the
"grotesque" images of the townspeople. The disembodied voice,
then, is not a purposely perverse power, but a narrative instrument
which, eventually embodied in Fellini's talking image, also expresses the child's original passion to venture into a fabulous visual
world.

Still, since the mature Fellini initiates the narrative adventure

into the "lost world" of his childhood through a categorical declara-
tion of the fall of contemporary potentialities for creativity, his
words inevitably give ironic utterance to the inherent deficiency of
the historical method as vehicle for the fulfillment of the enduring
aim in life itself. Wholly absorbed in an empty rhetoric that leads
him to ask about the fate of the clowns of his youth and about their
power to arouse the yearned-for "exhilaration," Fellini is not able to
narrate his way cinematically into a vision of the clowning that sur-
rounds his immediate present throughout the historical narration.
Because he is talking and not seeing, he cannot laugh when Maya
pulls the sheet of paper from the typewriter and rips it in half. He
can't see or laugh even later when she drops the still photographs of
old clowns or when she knocks heads with Gasperino as both try to
pick them up at the same time. At the Cirque d'Hiver, where Lina
(Alvaro's mother) sees herself in a mirror and where each crew
member looks into a different photograph of a clown, it is not surprising that Fellini is the one member of the crew who cannot
establish such a relation with an image of a clown. Only Fellini
clings to the dignity of dead words and of a past that is dead even
before he begins to inquire about it.

And indeed his failure to partake of the joy of the present is seen
time and again throughout the historical narration. For instance, he
cannot see himself as a participant in the world of the clowns when,
in the manner of the standard circus act, he, his entire crew, Pierre
Etaix, and Papa Gustav emerge from the small car on their way to
Annie Fratellini's. Because he is rapt in talk about the past with
Etaix, he cannot see Etaix as a white clown and Papa Gustav as an
Augusto when Papa Gustav, who carries the huge wooden crate
containing the special projector, stumbles and Etaix says to Fellini,
"It's all right, he likes it." Fellini cannot laugh when Papa Gustav
knocks his head on the projector table, when Roy plays with the
banjo, Alvaro with the trombone, and Gasperino with the twanging
instrument invented by one of the Fratellini brothers. Accordingly,
he cannot see that the Fratellini act which he has come to see in the
old black-and-white film is being performed before his very eyes
without the aid of the past and in living color. Nor is there any
evidence that Fellini even sees Lina, who with Annie's aid dons the
oversized cap, or Alvaro, who later tries on the blond wig. Instead,
Fellini is intent on seeing no more than the "rare" black-and-white

Fratellini short. It is his key, he believes, to the lost joy of his youth. But he can't laugh at himself when, "master director" that he is, he sheepishly admits that he knows nothing about projectors; and certainly he doesn't see anything to laugh about when the rare film fails to pass through the projector gate and burns.

At once blind to the immediate events of joy and in search of an idealized world, Fellini must incessantly interrupt the actions of the present in order to attend to a past in which the creative urge cannot actively participate. Just outside the ring of the Orfei circus, as he watches the lion cage being erected, Fellini asks an old man about the origins of the Augusto clown. The old man relates the story of a very clumsy servant named Augusto who became the inspiration for the first great Augusto clown, Jim Guillon. Again a link between life and art is established, this time by the nameless old man. The world in which Fellini seeks his joy abounds with narrators who can readily instruct him on how to make the connections between art and life.

The old man's story soon gives way to a visual narrative. But Jim Guillon's image is not that of a clown in the ring, but of a man on his deathbed who, having heard that Footit and Chocolat are in town, eludes the sleeping nun and goes to see their act. Amid the crowd in the stands, Jim laughs as the two clowns pull the chair out from under each other, as Footit tries to play the banjo and Chocolat the trumpet, and as both finally complete their musical number under the spotlight and leave the ring together.

It is clear that many of the components of the last sequence in *The Clowns* are present in the action that Jim sees. The union of the two clowns under the spotlight, the music, and even the fact that one of the clowns plays a trumpet, vividly show that this episode is an event that potentially satisfies the underlying passion through Jim's agency. Yet this narrative venture into the clown's world does not, and indeed cannot, end like the final sequence in the story, for as it ends, Jim is dead.

Nevertheless, the exploration of Jim's world exemplifies and embodies, in Jim's image, the pervasiveness of the search for freedom from a decadent vision. It becomes obvious that as a participant in the story Fellini partakes of the innocent exuberance that characterizes the Augusto clown. And since in the Antonet sequence that

follows almost immediately it is equally evident that Fellini displays
a sympathy toward the authoritarian qualities that define the white
clown, it becomes increasingly clear that the reconciliation of the
opposing characteristics that divide the Augusto from the white
clown is but another way of expressing the narrative progress toward
the unification of opposites.[12]

In Paris, where, according to the notes that Maya reads, clowning became "an art form," and where the crew has come to see
Tristan Rémy, "the greatest living circus historian," it is again clear
that Fellini seeks to "understand" laughter, that he searches for an
explanation of the new in terms of the old, and that he wishes to see
novelty only to the degree that he can abstract from it an essence
that will give permanence to and will thus in turn glorify the past.
For instance, at the Café Curieux, where Rémy and several retired
clowns gather around a table, Fellini inquires about the origins of
the white clowns' costumes. Immediately, almost as many different
historical versions are offered as there are men around the table.
From the divisive talk the story moves to the sequence where the
white clowns parade their attires in the ring. However, the ramp on
which the white clowns model their costumes runs almost the entire
length of the ring. It divides the ring in half, and from each side the
one group of clowns shouts insults at the other. Obviously they
argue as to whose costume is the most beautiful. Soon the camera
moves up close to the distorted, angry white faces of the clowns.
Then it cuts back abruptly to an equally close shot of the old clowns
as they, along with Rémy, also argue about who is historically right
and who is wrong.

At this instant the camera is little more than an extension of
Fellini's persistent effort to regain his lost joy through the agency of
words. As such, it is wholly consistent with the historical narration
that the camera should deny its delight with images and attend to
the divisive dialectics of the historian and of the retired clowns. The
visual powers are made to do the bidding of the intellect, and the
camera can see nothing but moving mouths. Turning away from the
image results only in furthering the disjunction between the esthetic aim and the objects of its fulfillment.

Therefore if the Jim Guillon sequence showed Fellini nothing
because the historical method prevented him from transcending the

vision of death, the sequence showing the white clowns' costumes also manifests the failure of the historical mode to achieve unity between the search and the passion that propels it. The present, this sequence has shown, is but a joyless repetition of an equally joyless past. Shortly after the argument Rémy asks Fellini, "Why do a film on clowns?" The "art," he claims, "is dead"; and he arrogantly asserts that it "deserved to end as it did." The mirthless historian and his negative narrative allegations become yet another burden that the esthetic aim must bear so long as it consents to the past as the exclusive vehicle for the attainment of the festive vision.

Eventually the crew finds its way to the nursing home where Captain Houcke, the ninety-three-year-old former circus impresario, lives. The claims of Houcke's nurses notwithstanding, Houcke says that he remembers nothing about the circus. This is particularly interesting since Houcke is also the man who says that were he still active he would "discover another Gigli and another Schipa," and that he would "create the circus of the future." But Fellini is not interested in Houcke's visions. He will not learn from this man who offers him a link between past, present, and future. The crew leaves as Houcke begins to sing in a feeble, broken voice. Rejecting Houcke as a senile old man, Fellini denies himself an opportunity to see that the "lost world" can be discovered by that passion to create which is itself embodied in the old man. Instead, Fellini seeks the reenactment of past joys in the old acts of other retired clowns, such as Charlie Rivel, and later, Père Loriot and Bario. Rivel talks about his birth in the circus and about how the government should institute a school for clowns. He talks intermittently in Spanish, Italian, and French, and all during his talk it is clear that the members of the crew are bored. Only Gasperino smiles, while both Maya and Alvaro yawn, and Roy is inattentive. Finally, when Charlie entertains the crew, he dons his red wig and round red nose and moans and cries as he plays the guitar. With nothing to see but boredom and sorrow, the camera cuts away from Rivel's wail.

After the Fratellini film burns, Fellini requests old photographs and scrapbooks. From these, the historical mode takes the story to the three Fratellini performances. The first takes place before pupils and nuns at a girls' school, the second before hospital patients, and the last before inmates in an insane asylum. Throughout these three acts there is a definite "progression" toward an increasingly somber mood on the part of the different audiences. The school girls are visibly delighted. At the hospital, however, only a few of the patients show signs of amusement. At the insane asylum no one laughs. As is evident in the last Fratellini performance, where the doctor takes over the brothers' act by hypnotizing the inmate who threatens the Fratellinis, several members of the audience themselves become clowns by acting out their own irrational energies. But even here no one laughs. The reenactment of the Fratellini performances illustrates the process of narrative degeneration that pervades the historical method. As the performances exhibit the exhaustion of possibilities for joy and freedom in the past, so does the historical pattern continue to unfold the unmistakably degenerative function of the past as a vehicle to display the energies of the underlying zest.

"They never laughed. Nobody laughed," says Père Loriot to Fellini as he relates his audience's response to his act in Rome. And indeed Loriot may well be speaking about what Fellini himself has been able to discover from the past and its relation to the present. For the nostalgic insistence on the past shows that memory is dead, unable to be impregnated with the contemporary world of joy. Fellini once more resorts to looking at black-and-white photographs—this time those of Loriot's dead wife. But by now looking at photographs cannot even lead to a fruitless recreation of the past such as was occasioned by looking at the Fratellini scrapbooks. To contradict Santayana, the more Fellini remembers the past, the more he is condemned to repeat it. It is no mere coincidence that Fellini finds himself drinking to the memory of Loriot's wife. The isolated past echoes its own hollowness.

And Bario, the last old clown visited by Fellini, says that he "can't forget the circus," but when he is asked about the circus of the present, he is quick to point out that the circus is dead. All that is left for Fellini is to visit the French television archives to view a rare film of Rhum, to whom Rémy refers as the greatest of all clowns.[13] But once again the idealized past proves incapable of enacting a regenerative vision. More than an abstraction made for cataloging purposes, "435 Series 12," the rare Rhum film, is an abstraction from the world of color. The black-and-white film points to the irreconcilability of opposites from which the historical method is unable to free itself. Immediately after the disappointingly short film, an almost desperate Fellini finds himself asking the curator, "Is that all? Are you sure?" In the "vast funereal atmosphere" of the French television building Fellini discovers that the joyless glimpse of Rhum is all that a subjectively isolated past will let him see. Laughter and joy, this narrative mode ironically illustrates, are not matters of historical knowledge, but potentialities to be explored with a zest that corresponds to the revelations of images in the present.

Fellini himself articulates best the final result of a historically oriented inquiry into a world of laughter and joy when he says at the end of the historical narration, "We felt disappointed. . . . Our journey had taken us nowhere. Maybe Rémy is right. Maybe the clown really is dead." Neither the little boy nor the mature man has seen anything that is "nice," anything that is joyful, anything in the past or the present which liberates the esthetic aim from the child's initial terror.

The enactment of Fischietto's funeral is the clearest indication of the esthetic aim's persistent thrust toward fulfillment. Even if it begins by perversely attempting to image death, the very presence of the images on the screen is evidence that what has died is not the world of clowning but the historical method. If the fundamental function of the funeral sequence were not to announce the birth of a new way to satisfy the creative urge, The Clowns would have ended with Fellini's elegy.

Still, since the artificial narrative method immediately follows Fellini's words, it is also obvious that this method attempts to foster the fruitless vision of the historical mode. Soon after the funeral begins, the ringmaster, who is referred to by one of the clowns as "the director," reprimands the rest of the clowns by asking harshly, "Don't you realize there's been a tragedy?" His words single him out as the bearer of the verbal "message" which the action in the ring is about to show to be hollow, just as the present has already begun to show that Fellini's own words lack the finality they pretend to have. Indeed, before "the director's" pronouncement, a clown, his feet in a bucketful of tears, tells the little old clown, "Your sorrow will refresh my feet." Thus contradicting both Fellini and "the director," this clown announces the powers for regeneration, for "refreshment," available even in a world shot through and through with the misery of intellectual narration.

Moreover, the actions that begin to unfold in the ring confirm the words of the clown with the tired feet and not those of Fellini or of "the director." In one of the first acts in the sequence, one clown squirts his beer over "the director," thus initiating the obstreperous action, vital to this narrative mode, consisting of undermining the pompously authoritative and manipulative inclinations of the narrative forces that stand in the way of a rebirth. The old clown, who is later to propel the story into its "genial" mode, walks casually away from a heavy fur coat which stays upright in its place. Sloughing off the rigid weight, he is now empowered to move freely about and eventually to display narrative powers which are not burdened by history or artifice. Shortly thereafter, Fischietto's widow joyfully primps before the mirror, preparing in effect not for the funeral, but for the eventual resurrection. As she is engrossed in making her image all the more appealing, she shows that there is no death within the ring. Also the son, a short old man in black with a long white beard, runs to the side of his dead father and changes hats with him and with other "mourners," blurring the distinctions between young and old, past and present, death and life, which had been attended to as intellectual categories of time by the historical narration.

Furthermore, two members of Fellini's crew actively participate in the events in the ring. Lina, who was the first member of the crew to see herself as a clown at Annie's, now attends to the widow, helping her get ready for the great occasion. Gasperino too is in the ring helping to fill the buckets with glue. Thus Gasperino is one of the clowns directly responsible for sticking the buckets of glue over Fellini's and the interviewer's heads. Both Gasperino and Lina, their passion to clown ignored by Fellini's oppressive voice throughout the historical narration, are now in the center of the action, themselves clowns beyond the control of Fellini, the "director."

But inasmuch as they are empowered to carry the story closer to the fulfillment of the pervading impulse, the most significant events during the artificial narration are to be found in numerous individual acts—having their antecedent in the scene in which the clown squirts beer over "the director"—in which particular images display their independence from controlling forces. For instance, when the white clown who drives the hearse orders his "horses" onward, one goes off by itself and refuses to continue, saying that it is over-worked. Later, as another elegy is delivered by another white clown, two of the horses, obviously bored by the oration, leave the yoke and sit on the edge of the ring while the driver screams, "Get back to your place!" The horses challenge the attempts of the driver to ascribe to them a "place," a fixed location, or a subordinate role. And still later, these same horses finally manifest their complete freedom from the driver when they dance with each other, celebrat-ing the outburst of color and the emergence of Fischietto from atop the giant Martini bottle. Again, when Fellini signals from outside the ring for the explosion of the special fireworks intended to ac-company the breakdown of the still camera that is about to photo-graph the performers in the ring, the fireworks fail to go off, only to explode by themselves as soon as Fellini gives up on them. The action, it is clear, will hold still neither on account of the tragic pronouncement nor in deference to the directorial intention that seeks to freeze, to kill, the motion.

When a clown tries to play the tuba, it makes the wrong sound; then, after he puts his head in the hole to inquire about the malfunc-tion, the tuba plays itself. Later, two tubas spew forth fireworks, and firemen pour water on each other, unable to control the fire hoses. Even the "inanimate" objects acquire a life of their own. All the action is composed of individual images that manifest their particu-lar method of narration and contribute to the fulfillment of the pervading passion.

But of all these events preceding the resurrection the action within the ring is most clearly beyond the boundaries of an extrane-ously imposed order when the mirror image of the clown who car-ries the wooden board ceases to do as the clown does and reveals its autonomy by failing to take its hat off and by mocking the "real" image. The image possesses an immanent power to generate an action that is free from all restrictive forces, even if one of these forces is that of an absolute, conceptual reality. In fact, the activity in the ring breaks out of the circle and declares its independence from both Fellini and his intellectual interviewer when Fellini, now an authority himself, is about to reduce the life in the ring to a "message" and gets a bucket of glue over his head. The action itself shows that there is no such thing as a derivatively real visual world, and that the images are the living embodiments of a narrative activity that is clearly meant to be lived and not controlled or contemplated.

Toward the end of the artificial narrative sequence, when Fischietto bursts from atop the giant Martini bottle and flies through the color streamers, it cannot be asserted with any degree of accuracy that Fellini the "director" has staged the clown's rebirth. "Fischietto," it is crucial to remember, is in the beginning of the sequence a dummy. By the end, however, he is very much a "creature of flesh and blood" who owes his transformation to no extraneous imaginative power. Thus the images assert their freedom, transform themselves into fluent narrative energies, and unfold their inherent wealth of cinematic narrative possibilities for the satisfaction of their own and the world's esthetic craving. Indeed, at the end of the second narrative mode the creation appears complete, the esthetic aim fulfilled, until Fellini's disembodied voice abruptly concludes the unified vision, saying, "Turn it off. It's over."[14]

All the world is an image, is many images with as many esthetic cravings—all the world, that is, but Fellini the "director." And yet this abstract fragment, this alienated narrative power, reclaims its supremacy over the visual world. Wickedly insistent on having its way with the life in the ring, the voice commands the end of the action like an angry god envious of a glorious achievement in which he alone has failed to participate, like a deity conscious that his world has disobeyed his absolute pronouncement on the fall, and yet aware that man's image has created itself. As a direct result of its intellectual refusal to be incorporated into the celebration of the rebirth, the voice proclaims the death of the nascent occasion. It draws attention to itself as the terminus of the process of concrescence between the narrative and the creative zest; it asserts that the visual events in the ring are mere artifice and that it can easily dispense with them.

Accordingly, the potentialities for the convergence of a narrative mode with the esthetic yearning remain unrealized; the two are thoroughly polarized, in fact. In affirming its egotistical penchant for control over the life in the ring, the voice fails to exhibit its power to consummate the enduring passion. Therefore the transition into the third and final narrative mode is more than an arbitrary shift to an alternate route for the satisfaction of the esthetic yearning. It is accordingly futile to search for a logical cause to explain the emergence of the genial narrative mode beyond the fundamental desire of the enduring impulse to express itself in terms totally harmonious with the cinematic present.

The life of the individual is the greatest narrative authority. Narrative is at its truest, its most beautiful, its best when it is the result of the individual passion for expression. It is not Fellini as the visually timid child nor as the mature intellectual-historian nor as "director"—nor, it goes without saying, is it Pierre Etaix nor Rémy nor the retired clowns—but a clown, single, individual, and active, who quickens the power for the convergence of method and aim. During that part of the funeral sequence when all the clowns run frantically around the ring, the little old clown leaves the ring exhausted, but even then he watches the action and applauds it with visible delight. Subsequently, after Fellini's voice signals the end of all possibilities arising from Fischietto's resurrection, the clown addresses Fellini. One of the basic feats of this particular form of narration enacted by the clown is that the revelation potentially available to the child in his encounters with both the pony trainer and with the ringmaster bearing the Siamese twins is now freely allowed to flow and to fulfill itself. Like the boy, Fellini too becomes the camera. More accurately still, the self, the "I" which has been throughout so frustrated in its search for joy, dies as a controlling force and gives way to imaginative vision as the vehicle for growth with and within the creation.

The genial narration begins verbally. The clown's first words, however, express neither the boy's terror nor the mature Fellini's recurring nostalgic uncertainties nor the dark pessimistic assertions made by both Rémy and Etaix. After the resurrection the clown says, "I liked it very much." Unlike the words of the disembodied voice which arrogantly expressed disdain for the rebirth, the clown's words attest to his capacity to embrace the events in the ring as an occasion for joy. Consequently, in addition to having the capacity for participation in the events within the center of the action, the clown also testifies to his power for exhilaration as a spectator. And there is still another even more significant dimension to the genius of this clown. For he can grow beyond his performer-spectator phase and generate the narrative that finally fulfills the esthetic aim. Since there is now no verbal counterpart to the clown (Fellini's voice dies for good when the clown begins his narration), the heretofore dominant dialectical methodology—whether in the form of the historical mode or in that of the artificial bifurcation between life and art—is immediately eliminated as a narrative power.

As Fellini is told by Rémy that clowning is dead, so is the clown told by the ringmaster, in the story that the clown relates, that Fru-Fru, his partner, is dead. Fellini's intellectual predispositions had allowed him to accept the dictates of the old authorities. The clown, on the other hand, questions the finality of the words that pronounce the death of his partner. He says, "Well, I wouldn't give up [looking for Fru-Fru]." The fact is that the clown embodies the esthetic urge in a far greater degree than Fellini has so far. The difference in degree of intensity of the enduring passion is therefore another way of accounting for the difference in narrative modes. And again one of the major factors accounting for the difference between the clown's narrative achievements and Fellini's is the fact that whereas Fellini's narrative inclinations have throughout prevented him from seeing "the clown" any way but generically, the individual clown locates the source of his genial narration in another single, individual, discrete clown. Thus whereas Fellini's narrations have entailed a relation of "I-to-them"—with the "I" as the primordial classifying narrative entity—the clown's narration is "image-to-image." The discrete image whose life the clown narrates is the image which in turn narrates the clown's life into the vision of joy. Narrative reciprocity is accordingly the great distinguishing feature of the genial narration.

Like both Fellini the participant and Fellini the "director," then, the clown has a method for discovery. But this maker of joy has, by comparison, an infinitely more profound wisdom, for it is transparently clear to him that the way into regeneration is through an endlessly renewable esthetic experience, and it is just as clear to him that his art has the strength and the vitality of life. "If [Fru-Fru] is dead, how will I find him?" he asks. And he answers himself: "So I began to call him with the trumpet." The clown relates a direct and immediate method for the liberation from death as ultimate fact.

The fundamental value of the genial narration is therefore summarily discovered in the vision of a newly acquired innocence. The method's inherent freedom from subjectivism, from the past, and from the divisiveness of words is in turn a bold freedom—a power to act with the life of the clown, to envision birth in unity, and to participate fully in the vision. The genial mode thus enables relations to be made by and for the moving image in color, and by and for esthetic experience as a living value. As the new method requites the enduring passion, so does that impulse for joy satisfy the most subtle actions of the clown and his method. The past is now released into the present; the enduring aim, once expressed only through words, is liberated to rejoice in the actions of the image. Nothing is rejected; rather, all is transformed by the desire to partake of a wealth of life which none of the preceding narrative methods could have revealed.

Extending the method for the vision of rebirth enacted by the old clown, the camera eye sees the miraculous creation of an image of a clown playing a trumpet at the far end of the stands. Then, following the spotlight to the opposite end of the stands, the eye sees a second clown reply, as it were, to the first as he plays the second bar of "Ebb Tide." Soon the eye moves back to the first clown, seeing him begin his descent into the ring as he continues to play the trumpet. As the eye continues its movement from one clown to the other, seeing them approach the center of the ring, it is clearly the eye which now generates a new phase of the genial narration by fleshing out, by particularizing, the visual possibilities residing in the music.

And as important as the initiative the eye takes in transforming the narrative mode by visualizing music is the fact that the eye also initiates the process of unification of which it too is now a vital part. For the images of the clowns, though seen, are in the beginning polarized. Indeed, not only are they spatially separated—immobile, as they are, at the opposite ends of the stands—but they also are separated by virtue of the tensions between life and death, the past and the present, and life in and outside the ring as articulated by the clown who initiates the genial narration. Thus while the individual clown announces the basic relation-making process, and the two clowns who play the trumpets carry the new mode forward by embodying the clown's narrative passion, it now belongs to the eye to assimilate the possibilities for satisfaction available in these two phases of the genial mode and to carry those possibilities to their consummation. Consequently, the completion of the musical piece

by the two clowns is but a unit in the total convergence of creative
forces present in the last scene.

Even as the two clowns stand in the center of the ring, still under
the bright spotlight, they never look at each other, they never discover each other visually. The enveloping power, confirming both
the completion of the piece and the union of the two clowns as
formative elements in the total act of concretion, is the indivisible
relationship between the eye and the ring. In short, the eye cen-
tralizes the action by entering the realm previously denied to it
and by discovering that *it* is the power over the disjunct and the
polarized. The eye attests to its capacity not only to see, but to see
and to create the good. It is now therefore clearer than ever that the
eye is not merely an optical eye, but an extension of the esthetic aim
itself. Creating the living, mature image from the dead and the
embryonic, the eye meets and then transcends the narrative challenge of the ringmaster's question. Once seen directly, the image is
"nice," beautiful, good. Since narration itself is its essence, the
esthetic aim becomes the supremely moral event, namely, the process of enacting an ever-growing union between life and art.

United by the spotlight and completing their musical piece, the
two clowns walk out of the ring. They fade out and then the spotlight
also fades out. But the ring remains—empty, as empty as at the
instant the child first sees it, yet full of the energies potentially
conducive to a new discovery of and delight in images. Beyond the
immediate satisfaction of the esthetic aim and even beyond the
resulting moral triumph of the creative spirit, there remain boundless narrative possibilities for a world of cinematic values at the
center of which is the liberated image ever offering itself to the new
narrative commitment, and ever displaying its existence in the
plastic present, where it is at once the source of liberation from the
heaviness of human suffering and the origin of the freedom to seek
the supreme and ever-present facts of moral and imaginative birth
in the visible creation.

EPILOG

The vegetation still abounds with forms.
WALLACE STEVENS

An important aspect of the genius of the clowns' resurrection is to be found in the direction of their motion. They descend from the highest place in the circus, join under the spotlight at the lowest possible place, and walk away from the open-ended ring. Resurrection, rebirth, need not be transcendental; the resurrection at the end of the genial mode is much more humanistically appealing than the one at the end of the artificial mode. Fischietto's resurrection, for all its liberating and anarchic exuberance, takes place on high. Fischietto is accordingly separated from the very world to which he owes his life. Suspended by the cable fastened to his waist, he becomes a sort of impotent latter-day *deus ex machina*, looking down on creation yet hopelessly isolated from it. He is unable to participate further in the joy created by the self-unified action of the ring. As a consequence, Fischietto, like Fellini the "director" himself, is separated from the source and origin of a life that offers continual salvation and regeneration. Therefore, in comparison with the resurrection in the genial mode, Fischietto's resurrection contains its own element of artificiality.

The descent of the two clowns, constituting as it so clearly does a descent into the world, announces that the pervading spirit of generation and birth—the fulfillment of the most intensely human narrative passion—is in the kingdom of this world. The two clowns complete their musical piece in perfect harmony. As they fade out, they are just out of the ring. The ring, the microcosmic setting for the festive occasion, opens up into the greater world, into life itself.

The Clowns therefore attests to the fact that life is not just art, but art about art. Thus the fundamental cinematic value of *The Clowns* resides in its capacity to announce the union of the divine and of the human, of salvation and life, in the world—in the only world there is because there need not be any other. God's creativity, which is his supremely moral attribute, inheres in the individual image. It lives through the narrative acts of images. Accordingly, the relation between God and the world, which is traditionally the ultimate expression of ideal opposites, finds its living synthesis in the cinematic image that creates both itself and the world as it acts. The image of the individual—without name or identity, without self-concept or substance, without, in a word, character—has become theurgy incarnate, has itself become the new man because divinity now lives actively as a narrative value in and through the agency of such images.

The question might nonetheless be asked: Pray, where, at the end of *The Clowns*, is this new image of man? For that matter, it may be asked, Where is such an image in *Director's Notebook*, in *Seven Beauties*, in *Blowup*? After all, *Director's Notebook* ends with a fade-out; *Seven Beauties* with Pasqualino's perverse verbal abuse of the image of his salvation and with his willful transcendence of his condition as an image for the sake of becoming a deified voice; *Blowup* with the photographer's disappearance in the green expanse; *The Clowns* itself with the fade of the two clowns just as they are outside the ring.

The questions as to where such images are—which might well be extended to encompass a question as to where such images are going—are legitimate humanistic questions, for they amount to inquiries into the relationship between cinematic narration and life itself. But if all they seek by way of an answer is what happens to the image of man within each particular movie, that is, if they are asked only "intensively," the questions are not quite properly asked. In order that the questions bear directly on the relationship between cinematic values and life, they must be asked "extensively"—that is, the inquiries must bear in mind the growth of narrative and cinematic values as powers able to beget humanistic values. Otherwise such legitimate and relevant questions would be asking the movies to bestow an *archetypal image* on a mind preoccupied with otherworldliness. And at the same time such questions would implicitly demand a theory such as would explain the humanistic ideal that inheres in such an image. Where is the Good? they would ask. It would then be fitting to answer along with William James, "All Goods are disguised by the vulgarity of their concomitants, in this work-a-day world; but woe to him who can only recognize them when he thinks them in their pure and abstract form!" It is not within the power of common events that move, change, and grow, to answer questions dialectically and definitively about their existence in time and place or about the "purpose" of their narrative processes. They might just answer that they are nowhere. They might just answer that they are anywhere. Perhaps even everywhere. But none of those answers would satisfy a teleologically biased question, no matter how humanistic the spirit of the question may seem to be.

It is, however, very much within the power of such images to proclaim the world as an open-ended phenomenon, to reveal it morally and esthetically as, in Einstein's phrase, "finite yet unbounded." Better yet, it is within the moral power of such narratives to affirm with John Dewey that "growth itself is the only moral 'end.'" In a world where there are as many images of man as there are men narrating within each discrete moment, each image is the disclosure of a new man living his temporal existence as the creator of a new world. That is "all" that the cinematic image of man can do by way of answer.

Achilles' obsession with the glory, reaped of battle, whereby future generations might come to know and sing of him; Oedipus's exile from Thebes devoted to the exclusive purpose of narrating his tragedy; Hamlet's dying plea to Horatio that he report him and his cause aright—these are examples of the narrative necessities of the precinematic epoch. Where there was no verbal narration to perpetuate a relation, a life, there was thought to be no value in the life itself.

But now the continual disappearance, the "death," of one particular image from the screen is nothing less than the continual announcement of another's birth; it is nothing less than the appearance of a new image of man—onscreen or in life—which is itself integrally, the result of its relations to other images, and the bearer of immanent potentialities to beget more images, more life. Such an ever-changing, creative image is the narrative of the world itself in the act of revealing all its complex novelty in the perishing event that cannot help but live, as both actuality and potentiality, forever. To repeat a phrase made in relation to *Director's Notebook*, the new image of man in his cinematic world is "the perfectly incomplete event."

But how exactly does such an image live? How exactly does it grow? To answer that it lives and grows exactly as it does in each of its narrational moments ought to suffice. But the imagined question demands more critical respect for the imagined inquisitor. The first thing to say, then, is that in order to discover exactly how such an image of man lives, it has to be seen in a unique relation, namely, in the particular narrative function of the cinematic event and in the welter of possibilities for value inherent in the function of the cinematic event. Either the contemporary mind keeps pace with a world of continuous action or it dies. For the image of man is no mere "imitation" anymore. The image is man himself, the "creature of flesh and blood."

Accordingly, one of the powers contributing to the clarification of the growth of cinematic values is the heuristic function of thought begotten of the image itself. For such is the thought which eagerly embraces the living act and seeks to elicit as many values as reside in a particular phase in the growth of man's image. And the image, now unveiled—and thus no longer in need of criticism by comparison to ideas, concepts, or archetypes—itself leads into its own adventures and discoveries.

Yet the heuristic value of criticism extends beyond eliciting the human worth of the ever-fresh. The greater critical obligation is to the imperative to return the image of man to a condition whereby it can continue to disclose its actualizations of and its potentialities for value. In this way, without being moralistic or dogmatic, both the narrations of the images and the thought that emerges out of them become moral events inasmuch as they urge the further exploration of methods whereby both can be made more and more appealing to that one, ultimate humanistic value—the free and adventurous search for new values wherever they may be found, in whatever movie, in whatever moment of life. Thus it is that man's image lives.

Man lives as he narrates. He cannot help but narrate. Narration and life are synonymous. Thus man is no more and no less than what he narrates. In the precinematic epoch it was all but inevitable for man to narrate himself out of the world. His transcendental aspirations, only slightly tempered by an intellect disturbed by the finite and the temporal, led him to find refuge outside the world, led him to seek solace in ideas and archetypes, first causes and substances, communal heroes and omnipotent gods, transcendental egos and conceptual categories, inflexible theories and philosophical doctrines. The mode of narration reflected his fear of change, his reluctance to grow morally and esthetically. He therefore lived by the word, gave preeminence to the fixed, and ascribed worth to the knowledge of the fixed as an end in itself; he assigned the greater glory to subjectivism and *ex nihilo* invented a masterful will. He gave primacy to these narrative values because they could transport him to a kingdom not of this world, but also because the liberated image was not a narrative alternative.

The movies, and especially the movies of the postwar era, ushered in a new narrative possibility, and thus a fresh alternative for a new life in the world. And as if that were not enough, the advent of the movies promised to dispel intellectual man's most entrenched fears by offering him all that he had hoped for and much more, and by ennobling him that he might fulfill his fondest dreams here, in this world. Among so many movies, the four discussed in this essay are but concrete instances, specific models, of the function of new narrative discoveries in relation to man's primordial impulse to narrate. They are but four living instances disclosing the awesome complexity of a new world in which a new man is needed as creator and participant—not that he may be master over it, but that he may rejoice to see the new image of his own making as it continues to grow into new visions of human and divine wisdom.

Appendix: The Episodes in
DIRECTOR'S NOTEBOOK

1. At the decaying Mastorna set
2. At the Mastorna prop room, a "graveyard," as Fellini calls it
3. The trip to the Colosseum, ending with "the man with the sack"
4. Giulietta Masina, the deleted sequence from *Nights of Cabiria,* and Cabiria's own encounter with "the man with the sack"
5. The "Romans" Fellini first saw as a young boy at the movies
6. The Genius episode and the trip to the cemetery
7. The professor of archeology and the subway ride
8. Appian Way whores sequence (Fellini absent; Marina Boratto as verbal narrator)
9. At the beginning of the Appian Way, where Marcello Mastroianni lives
10. Mastroianni/Mastorna screen-test sequence
11. Slaughterhouse episode
    (a) "Preface" by English-speaking narrator
    (b) Entrance into the slaughterhouse
    (c) Stone busts of ancient Romans
    (d) Outside the slaughterhouse with the butchers as gladiators, senators, emperors, etc.; also the shy woman and Caterina Boratto
12. Casting office sequence
13. On the set of *Fellini-Satyricon*

NOTES

CHAPTER 1

1. About the making of this movie Fellini writes: "I made *A Director's Notebook* ... very casually, to tell the truth, as if it was just something that I had to be free of. But that sketchiness, in the right sense of the word, *that haste and lightness made me feel very joyful. I felt I was walking faster, unhampered by luggage.... In other words, I saw the chance of doing something new*" (italics mine). *Fellini on Fellini,* trans. Isabel Quigley ([New York]: Delacorte Press, 1976), p. 116.

2. Obviously Stuart Rosenthal saw *Director's Notebook* as no more than a mock-up for later Fellini movies when he wrote in *The Cinema of Federico Fellini* (Cransbury, N.J.: A. S. Barnes, 1976): "*Fellini: A Director's Notebook* has several segments which appear in expanded versions in *Roma. Director's Notebook* was made for American television, presumably to give viewers an impression of how Fellini makes his films and where he gets his ideas. In the film, he visits the 'night people' in the Colosseum and then shows the 'Man with the Sack' sequence that was cut from *Nights of Cabiria*. It was in the Colosseum, he explains, that he originally met this strange philanthropist. By the same token, the traffic jam in front of the Colosseum and the views of Rimini are simply sketches for a film he has in mind. They are valuable because—after *Roma* was released—they show how Fellini eventually elaborated those germs of ideas into complex set-pieces" (p. 37). This passage is an example of the author's implicit critical disdain for *Director's Notebook* within the Fellini canon. On the other hand, Joseph McBride sees the inherent value of *Director's Notebook:* "[*Director's Notebook*] is a development, not a regression: this is a film about how a man breaks loose from his artistic inhibitions and finds the moral strength to move forward and work again." "The Director as Superstar," in *Federico Fellini: Essays in Criticism,* ed. Peter Bondanella (New York: Oxford University Press, 1978), p. 153. For a brief yet brilliant account of the creative significance of *Director's Notebook* as far as Fellini's cinematic career goes, see Walter C. Foreman, Jr., "The Poor Player Struts Again: Fellini's *Toby Dammit* and the End of the Actor," in *The 1977 Film Studies*

Annual: Part One, Explorations in National Cinemas (Pleasantville, N.Y.: Redgrave Publishing Co., 1977), pp. 111–23.

3. For an example of "formal reflexivity" in relation to one of Fellini's own movies, see Christian Metz, "Mirror Construction in 8½," in *Film Language: A Semiotics of the Cinema*, trans. Michael Taylor (New York: Oxford University Press, 1974), pp. 228–34.

4. Hereafter, unless otherwise indicated, any textual reference to "Fellini" will be to the participant in the action of *Director's Notebook*, without special regard to his function as verbal narrator, image, or creative eye. Thus, allowing for latitude of terminology, these references to Fellini find themselves in perfect agreement with Peter Bondanella when he writes: "One expects 'serious' critical opinion from the late Pier Paolo Pasolini or Bernardo Bertolucci, but even the most serious of film critics often seems to view Fellini in the role Fellini himself provides for his spectators in such works as *Fellini: A Director's Notebook, The Clowns,* and *Roma*. But this role is simply that, a role—it is the *character* Federico Fellini portrayed by the *actor* Federico Fellini as manipulated by the *director* Federico Fellini. The role should not be confused with the man behind the camera." "Introduction," in *Federico Fellini: Essays in Criticism,* ed. Peter Bondanella, p. xii.

5. The dialog is from the original soundtrack, which is in English. The punctuation is my own. For the sake of convenience and clarity the following distinctions will be made in the text: "Mastorna" refers to the set or to "the City of Mastorna," as the hippie poet calls the set. "G. Mastorna" is the name of the would-be hero. "The Voyage of G. Mastorna" is the movie Fellini never made. I will, however, use "the Mastorna set" whenever it might be unclear whether the place or the hero's name is meant.

6. Despite himself, Fellini senses this growth when, very early in the story, he says, "A little while ago I came back to see all this again. It was more beautiful now, falling down and covered with weeds."

7. "Archaic" here has no pejorative meaning, even if the term is used to denote the traditional. It is a fitting term inasmuch as it is related to the first sentence of the Gospel according to John: "Ἐν ἀρχῇ ἦν ὁ λόγος."

8. Plato *Timaeus* 37.

9. *The Necessary Angel: Essays on Reality and the Imagination* (New York: Alfred A. Knopf and Random House, Vintage Books, 1942), p. 136.

10. Albert Einstein, *Relativity: The Special and the General Theory: A Popular Exposition,* 15th ed., trans. Robert W. Lawson (New York: Crown Publishers, 1961), p. 26; Alfred North Whitehead, *The Concept of Nature* (1920; reprint ed., Cambridge: The University Press, 1971), p. 66.

11. Aristotle *Poetics* 1450b.

12. Not only is Mastroianni a photographic abstraction because he is

made to stand still and because he is made to put on more weight, but also because he is made to look, at one point, like Guido in 8½. "Mastroianni, il cappello di 'Otto e mezzo' in testa, posa per la foto, con un lieve sorriso scettico." *Fellini TV: Block-notes di un regista, I clowns,* ed. Renzo Renzi (Bologna: Cappelli, 1972), p. 72.

13. *Necessary Angel,* pp. 151–52.

14. Henri Bergson, *The Creative Mind: An Introduction to Metaphysics,* trans. Mabelle L. Andison ([1913]; reprint ed., Secaucus, N.J.: Citadel Press, Wisdom Library, 1946), p. 98.

15. This new verbal narrator *describes.* He does not, as the English-speaking one, *demonstrate, interpret.* The appearance of the descriptive narrator and the implied death of the interpretive one are further disclosures of the new function of words in *Director's Notebook.*

16. *Fellini on Fellini,* p. 45.

CHAPTER 2

1. *Seven Beauties* is in many ways the narrative culmination of what Lina Wertmüller began with *The Seduction of Mimi.* In *The Seduction of Mimi, Love and Anarchy,* and *Swept Away. . . ,* the narrative crisis is as evident, but in none of these is it carried out to its breaking point as it is in *Seven Beauties.* John Simon has called *Seven Beauties* "an upward leap in seven-leagued boots that propels [Wertmüller] into the highest regions of cinematic art." "Wertmüller's 'Seven Beauties'—Call it a Masterpiece," *New York* 9, no. 5 (February 12, 1976): 24–31. Colin R. Westerbeck, Jr., seeing *Seven Beauties* within the Italian neorealist tradition, writes that "Pasqualino's return home at the end of *Seven Beauties* is neorealism brought to its ultimate, and perhaps logical, conclusion." "Beauties and the Beast: *Seven Beauties/Taxi Driver,*" *Sight and Sound* 45, no. 3 (Summer 1976): 134–39.

2. For examples of this narrative paradox in earlier Wertmüller movies, see Frank Burke, "Death-By-Abstraction: A Discussion of the Opening Sequence and Tunin's Demise in Wertmüller's *Love and Anarchy,*" in *1976 Film Studies Annual* (West Lafayette, Ind.: Purdue University Press, 1976), pp. 225–32; and Janet Staiger, "*Love and Anarchy:* An Unresolvable Paradox," ibid., pp. 288–301.

3. The Socialist doesn't literally die; he is condemned to twenty-eight years and four months in prison. But certainly he "dies" as a power able to rescue the story from its ideological chaos.

4. In *The Screenplays of Lina Wertmüller,* trans. Steven Wagner (New

York: Quadrangle, New York Times Books, 1977), the girl's name appears as Carolina. In the subtitled version of *Seven Beauties*, from which the dialog is taken, the girl has no name. Nor is the name Carolina in the Italian sound track itself. I will refer to her as "the girl" throughout the text, for not only is this the way in which the movie presents her but also because, pristine image that she is, she has no past, name, or identity, and thus more readily carries out her function as the discrete image that can potentially save Pasqualino. As for the other participants in the story, it is equally silly to refer to the Anarchist as Pedro, as the screenplay would have it, but as the movie does not. The man whose dream is "a new man" in "disorder" would himself scorn the name given him in the screenplay, which would make of him "the rock" (Peter). Also, the commandant is referred to as Hilde. She has no name. The appellation is merely an allusion to the commandant as Brünnhilde, a superfluous one especially in light of the saturation of Wagnerian music in the concentration camp sequences, and in light of the strains of *Die Walküre* that accompany her appearance onscreen.

5. Bruno Bettelheim, for whom, as a former concentration camp prisoner, it must have been painful even to see *Seven Beauties*, writes: "Nobody who is not fascinated by rape would dwell on [Pasqualino's rape of the sick woman and on his sexual encounter with the commandant], much less make one of [the scenes, presumably the latter] the centerpiece of the film." "Reflections (Concentration-Camp Survival)," *New Yorker*, August 19, 1976, p. 32. If he had not gotten trapped by his view of the movie as but an imitation (and a bad one at that, as he argues) of Nazi concentration camp life, Bettelheim could have seen that the courtroom sequence is "the centerpiece" because it teaches ever so much more than mere survival.

6. The screenplay translates the words of the song, which do not appear in the subtitles, as follows: "You've got to carry on living, not give a damn!"

7. The events in Pasqualino's life issuing from the court ruling in favor of his insanity plea are ultimately the perverse extension of Don Raffaele's demand that Pasqualino go to the Palonetto. The connection between the lawyer and Don Raffaele hardly needs mention in order to illustrate the callousness of both the criminal and the legal powers toward Pasqualino.

8. I use "intellect" here as a convenient term, but obviously Pasqualino is never the bearer of a culturally or historically acquired intellectualism, such as is exhibited by Francesco, the Anarchist, the Socialist, and, in a much more perverse way, by the commandant. And yet it is nothing but a raw, socially inherited "intellect" that allows Pasqualino to interpret the image, to classify it generically, and to rob it of its individuality.

9. Infinitely more repulsive than Pasqualino's survival instinct is the commandant's dream of a "master race." The irony of the anecdote of the

Greek resides precisely in the fact that the most repulsive figure in the story best articulates the motive force in Pasqualino's life.

10. Bruno Bettelheim writes that "'Seven Beauties' is confused—or, at least, confusing." "Reflections," p. 32. Bettelheim's statement would be more accurate were it not for his own confusion of Pasqualino's life as a concentration camp inmate with Pasqualino's narrative dilemma within *Seven Beauties* as a whole. The worlds in which Pasqualino lives, and with whose changes he fails to get in tune, are the source of *Pasqualino's*, not of the movie's, confusion.

11. All other images of men—whether those of the soldiers who parade before Hitler during the opening montage or of the German soldiers who capture Pasqualino and Francesco or of the officials in the courtroom or of the dead bodies and the prisoners in the concentration camp—lack visual particularization. The possible exceptions to this observation—the exceptions that prove the rule—appear in the scenes at the railway station and at the detention prison. In the former, the faces of the porters, and in the latter those of the other prisoners, are visually identifiable. But in both scenes Pasqualino is the dominant image. At the station he screams to the porters from atop the buggy. At the detention prison he imitates Mussolini and is separated from the others by a fence.

12. An assertion made by both Bettelheim and John Simon to the effect that postwar Naples is "a huge whorehouse" (Bettelheim) as a result of the presence of "Yankee liberators" (Simon), is superficial associationism. Both critics forget that by the time of the courtroom sequence all the sisters and all the other young women—visually identifiable as Pasqualino's girlfriends—are already whores. The pimp is the lawyer. And the women in the courtroom gallery are the only women seen previously in the streets of Naples. Now the fact—documented in neorealist movies such as de Sica's *Shoeshine* and Rossellini's *Paisan*—of prolonged American presence in postwar Italy is perhaps what prompts both Simon and Bettelheim to make such remarks about Americans as pimps. But according to the details of the story their remarks are in error. Above all, Simon's and Bettelheim's classification of the girl as "whore"—which amounts to an implicit identification with Pasqualino—ignores the fact that in postwar Naples the girl is about to make the transition from a world of materialistic necessity to the one of spiritual freedom that she is "ready" for but that Pasqualino's narrative perversity aborts.

13. The reference is to Henri Bergson, *Creative Evolution*, trans. Arthur Mitchell (1911; reprint ed., Westport, Conn.: Greenwood Press, 1975). See especially, pp. 182-97. There Bergson argues that of the two classes of animals with a highly developed sense of social activity—that is,

the hymenopteron and man—the former fails to evolve creatively because it uses all of its energies to perpetuate the existing "social order" through mere quantitative addition.

CHAPTER 3

1. As it appears on the screen at the beginning, the movie's title is not "Blow-Up" or "Blow-up," but *Blowup,* one word. Despite the conventional usage of the hyphenated title even in the screenplay (*Modern Film Scripts: "Blow-Up": A Film by Michelangelo Antonioni* [New York: Simon and Schuster, 1970]), I will throughout use the one-word title, as an illustration, trivial though it no doubt is, of the movie's essential unity and of this essay's attempt to be faithful to it.

2. "The photographer" is the photographer. He is not, as many critics have him, "Hemmings," or even "H.," referring to the actor's name. Nor is he "Thomas," as the Simon and Schuster screenplay and several other critics have him. Nor is he "The Young Man," as the directions in the same screenplay sometimes call him. Since he is a visual skeptic and at times also given to voyeurism, the name Thomas would be fitting, but he is never named in the movie. His *identity,* however, is clearly that of *photographer.* In the park he says to the girl, "Some people are bullfighters. Some people are politicians. I'm a photographer." Toward the end, when Ron tells him, "I'm not a photographer," the photographer angrily replies, "I am!"

It is appropriate here to clarify my references to all the other nameless participants in *Blowup.* The girl in the park is referred to as "the girl," not as "Jane," as the screenplay has her in parentheses in the cast credits, much less as "Miss Redgrave," as some critics have called her. What the screenplay collectively calls "students" and the critics "clowns" or "revelers" or "mimes" and also "students" are here referred to as "mummers," a term which, it seems to me, is more suited than "mimes" to describe their function, especially at movie's end, as creators of a "dumb show." The first model (Verushka) will be known as "the model." The other five will be referred to in the plural, that is, as "the models." It is more convenient to refer to Bill's girlfriend as Patricia, as the screenplay has it, even though her name is never mentioned in the story either. The young girls will be called "nymphs," since their function in the action is to act as a cinematic version of "attendants" to a power which in the case of *Blowup* is the power of color, motion, and irrepressible creative action. The young woman who owns the antique shop will be referred to as the "antique-shop owner" so as not to confuse her with the girl. The older man with the girl at the park will be referred to as "the man." The mystery man, the young blond-haired man first seen outside the restaurant by Ron, is referred to as "the blond man" but ought not to be confused with the assassin seen lurking behind the fence in one of the blow-ups.

3. The fact that Antonioni had the grass painted so that it would appear even greener is an incidental indication of the importance of color in *Blowup*.

4. "Almost exclusively," because during the sequences in which the photographer clips his enlargements of the photographs of the park next to each other and ponders their significance, the camera follows, for the most part, the sequential arrangement of the photographs and is for the most part aligned with the photographer's vision.

5. I deliberately avoid the use of *objective* to refer to the world of color and of *subjective* to refer to the photographer's world. Such a distinction is archaic and cumbersome because it is so steeped in the vague usage of different philosophical positions. When I do use the terms it is always in a deliberately oversimplified way, when the more specialized terminology has done most of its work. The use of the word *reality* to refer to the world of color and of *illusion* to refer to the photographer's world is deplorable, however much it may have been used in the criticism of *Blowup*. "Everything real," writes William James, "must be experienceable somewhere, and every kind of thing experienced must somewhere be real."

6. Antonioni has said that one of *Blowup*'s "chief themes" is "to see or not to see properly the true value of things." "Antonioni—English Style" (an interview on *Blowup*) in *"Blow-Up": A Film by Michelangelo Antonioni*, p. 14. Some critics have confused the cinematic with the photographic in *Blowup*, therefore finding it impossible "to see the true value of things" inasmuch as the photographic and the cinematic are contrasting, indeed conflicting, narrative modes. See, for instance, Roy Huss, "Introduction," in *Focus on "Blow-Up,"* ed. Roy Huss (Englewood Cliffs, N.J.: Prentice-Hall, 1971), p. 5; and for a particularly vague example, Max Kozloff, *"The Blow-Up,"* in *Focus on "Blow-Up,"* p. 59. Two essays that compare the Julio Cortázar story with Antonioni's movie exhibit a far keener sense of the narrative tensions between the photographic and the cinematic: "The tension between photography and written narrative in Cortázar becomes a tension between photography and cinematography in Antonioni." Henry Fernández, "From Cortázar to Antonioni: Study of an Adaptation," in *Focus on "Blow-Up,"* p. 166. "[In] the Antonioni version, . . . as the photographer comes to acknowledge the defeat of his previous manner of seeing and of being, he manages to effect . . . the beginnings of change within himself." Marvin D'Lugo, "Signs and Meanings in *Blow-Up*: From Cor-

tázar to Antonioni," *Literature/Film Quarterly* 3, no. 1 (Winter 1975): 23-29. See also Charles Eidsvik, *Cineliteracy: Film among the Arts* (New York: Random House, 1978), p. 219.

7. "But [*Blowup*]," writes one critic, "ends not tight and complete, but loosening and incomplete—in drama and activity. The latter part seems the foundation of another film (perhaps one already made by another director)." F. A. Macklin, "*Blow-Up*," in *Focus on "Blow-Up*," p. 38.

8. See, for example, Jean Clair, "The Road to Damascus: *Blow-Up*," in *Focus on "Blow-Up*," p. 54; Marsha Kinder, "Antonioni in Transit" in *Focus on "Blow-Up*," p. 84; and Charles Eidsvik, *Cineliteracy*, p. 226. Arthur Knight seems to see the ambiguity in *Blowup* as a value when he writes, "The very ambiguity of [Antonioni's] imagery in *Blow-Up* the young people find stimulating, provocative, exciting. Small wonder that Hollywood's film makers, still wedded to the written script derived from a literary source, find *Blow-Up* so difficult to accept. It opens vistas for a kind of cinema that they can neither understand nor hope to emulate. But by being so far out in front, it proves the umbrella under which undoubtedly more such films can and will be made—and is, therefore, not merely a challenge but a threat to much of what exists today." "Three Encounters with *Blow-Up*," in *Focus on "Blow-Up*," p. 69. In this context, there is no appreciable difference between what Knight calls ambiguity and I possibility.

9. "The sequence," Antonioni has said, "is neither erotic nor vulgar. It's fresh, light and—I hope—funny. I can't stop people finding a shocking element in it, but I needed this scene in the film and I didn't want to give it up because it might displease some people." "Antonioni—English Style" in "*Blow-Up*": *A Film by Michelangelo Antonioni*, p. 16.

10. The dialog is taken from the sound track of *Blowup*. I have relied on "*Blow-Up*": *A Film by Michelangelo Antonioni* only to the extent that in the screenplay the dialog, for the most part extremely accurate, helps to make the sound track more intelligible. The punctuation, however, is my own, not the screenplay's.

11. The body is in the park when the photographer takes the photograph of the distant image of the woman as she stops by the clump of bushes (just before she disappears on the other side of the hill). The body is present in front of the photographer—though he doesn't see it—when he pins the enlargement on one of the walls. This is the photograph that he looks at upon awakening after the romp with the nymphs. That the photographer sees the body only after the romp is no reason the viewer should not be able to affirm beyond doubt that he (the viewer) has seen it before. After all, the viewer is, or at least should be, visually aligned with the cinematic, not with the photographic, camera. At least one critic has made much of the need to acknowledge that the body is there before the photographer sees it.

See Charles Thomas Samuels, "'The Blow-Up': Sorting Things Out," in *Focus on "Blow-Up,"* p. 19.

12. For an interesting analogy between the photographic mode of narration and the scientific method in their relations to the narration of "truth" in *Blowup,* see Charles Eidsvik, *Cineliteracy,* p. 221.

13. "But the crowning irony of the scene, and the proof that Hemmings' progress is gratuitous, is that these two debauched little girls, numb as statues, seem to harbor one disappointment: they still haven't had their pictures taken!" Hubert Meeker, "Blow-Up," in *Focus on "Blow-Up,"* p. 49.

14. Carey Harrison, *"Blow-Up"* in *Focus on "Blow-Up,"* p. 41.

15. "'During [the making of *Red Desert*],' Antonioni says, 'I worked a lot with a telephoto lens in order to get flattened perspectives, so that I could tie together people and objects and make them seem pasted one on top the other. Nothing like that [in *Blowup*]. On the contrary, I have been trying to deepen the perspective, to put air between persons and things.'" "Antonioni in the English Style: A Day on the Set," in *Focus on "Blow-Up,"* p. 10.

16. *Oxford English Dictionary,* s.v. "perspective," gives this derivation: "[ad. late L. *perspectiv-us* (Boeth.),...]." If Boethius is indeed responsible for coining the word, it makes all the more sense within the scope of this chapter. Boethius was the consummate transcendentalist shortly after the fall of the Roman Empire.

17. The Italian masters placed the dominant, otherworldly image in the point of perspective, thus attracting the earthly eye to the "heavenly" image.

18. *The Notebooks of Leonardo Da Vinci,* comp. and ed. Jean Paul Richter, 2 vols. (New York: Dover, 1970), 1: 30. To avoid misleading the reader I have removed the brackets that Richter used around the second and third paragraphs.

19. This isn't the first time the viewer has had the opportunity to see the park. It is to the back of the photographer, the treetops swaying, attracting the eye, while the photographer snaps pictures of the antique shop.

20. The first time the girl and the man are seen is when the camera pans away from the photographer to follow the flight of one of the pigeons. The heads of the girl and the man are in the foreground.

21. For a partial explanation of the way in which the fragments of the photographer's world work only within a particular context, see Marsha Kinder, "Antonioni in Transit," in *Focus on "Blow-Up,"* p. 84.

22. I am indebted to the thought of William James for this observation. "In actual mosaics," writes James, "the pieces are held together by their bedding, for which bedding the Substances, transcendental Egos, or Abso-

lutes of other philosophies may be taken to stand. In radical empiricism there is no bedding; it is as if the pieces clung together by their edges, the transitions experienced between them forming their cement." *Essays in Radical Empiricism* (1912; reprint ed., Gloucester, Mass.: Peter Smith, 1967), p. 86. This notion of James is essential in many respects for the clarification of the manner in which the photographer's ego supplies the "bedding" between the photographs.

23. There is no effort here to include in the enumeration of the photographs those shots that the movie camera takes independently of the photographer's eye when it zooms in to some of the photographs. It is difficult to determine whether these zoom-ins and close-ups are totally different photographs or only different angles of them. The zoom-ins and the different angles, however, are important because they reveal the camera's willingness to explore the photographic mode. Cf. *"Blow-Up": A Film by Michelangelo Antonioni*, pp. 89-90.

24. See Max Kozloff, "The Blow-Up," in *Focus on "Blow-Up,"* p. 58.

25. "In a television interview with me, Antonioni said that Miss Redgrave read the script and wanted to play the part because—he lifted his hand in a gesture of placement on the screen—'*Sta li.*'

"'She stands there'; she has no explanations, no antecedents, no further consequences in the hero's life. I take this to mean that she is ... an event rather than a person ... and therefore perfectly consonant with the film." Stanley Kauffmann, "A Year with *Blow-Up,*" in *Focus on "Blow-Up,"* p. 76.

CHAPTER 4

1. I am indebted to W. R. Robinson for this remark. Robinson's observation, in an essay devoted mostly to *L'Avventura*, deserves to be quoted at some length in order to establish more clearly the relevance of his remark on "character" to *Blowup*. He writes: "For most viewers the movies remain a dramatic encounter, that is, a confrontation of character with character. . . . [Viewers] draw their life's blood in movies, as they do in everyday affairs, from the interaction between themselves and others as conventional public personalities. Such a perception and response to movies carries inherent within it a resistance to change in the outer form of man or in the external relations between men. When that resistance receives sufficient provocation to blossom into anxiety, any hint of human evolution in the movies get virulently attacked in the name of character for departing from the moral status quo. . . . Now 'character' specifies exactly what the term means etymologically, 'an engraved mark or brand.' It designates the rigid properties that a man bears indelibly, like the mark of Cain, through-

out his existence. That means that character is that part of him that has an enduring identifiability, a reliable stability, and predictability. For this reason character is that part of him that can be named. And since it can be named, it dwells in names—in titles or functions and roles—and thrives on words—in beliefs and ideologies, or intellectual stances and philosophical positions." "The Movies as a Revolutionary Moral Force, Part 2," *Contempora* 2, no. 1 (1972): 27. For a similar though not quite as incisively developed remark on "character" in *Blowup* and *Zabriskie Point*, see T. J. Ross, "Cool Times," in *Focus on "Blow-up,"* ed. Roy Huss (Englewood Cliffs, N.J.: Prentice-Hall, 1971), p. 98.

2. In all fairness to Antonioni's imaginative growth it must be said that in the beginning of *Zabriskie Point*, which he made after *Blowup*, the central male image, Mark, immediately walks away from a world of political talk and abstraction and singles himself out as an individual. Mark's fate, however, unlike that of Daria, the true protagonist of *Zabriskie Point*, is in net effect quite similar to the photographer's. Thus it is Daria who becomes the embodiment of the new individual narrative energies. For an excellent discussion of the evolution of the individual in *Zabriskie Point*, see Frank Burke, "Antonioni's Commitment to Daria and Creative Revolution," *1976 Film Studies Annual* (West Lafayette, Ind.: Purdue University Press, 1976), pp. 233–50.

3. Again, as in chapter 1, the reference to Fellini throughout the text of the present chapter is to Fellini as a participant in the action of *The Clowns*. The only difference is that in *The Clowns* there are three distinct "roles" played by Fellini—the "participant," the "historical narrator," and the "director," the last presiding over Fischietto's funeral.

4. The little old clown's name in the Italian screenplay is Fumagalli. Toward the end of the artificial narration, when this clown comes out of the ring exhausted, Fellini addresses him as Fumagalli. But his name doesn't appear in the subtitles nor is it sufficiently repeated in the soundtrack to make obvious the old clown's identity. I will therefore refer to him as "the old clown," or just "the clown," and will do so always in a context such that his own narrative feat may be credited to his fundamentally identity-less image.

5. Throughout a large portion of the sequence the child's back is in the immediate foreground, at the edge of the ring. It is thus clearer that, beholding and confirming the action from the same relation to the ring, the camera functions as the boy's eye.

6. The dialog is from the subtitled version of *The Clowns*. The punctuation is my own.

7. "The grotesque work of art," writes one critic, "evokes an estranged world which defies our powers to explain its coherence and order, one

which disobeys the common sense laws of cause and effect which we have come to expect of reality." William J. Free, "Fellini's *I Clowns* and the Grotesque," in *Federico Fellini: Essays in Criticism*, ed. Peter Bondanella (New York: Oxford University Press, 1978), p. 190. Free is unquestionably accurate inasmuch as he senses that the narrative thrust of *The Clowns* propels the story beyond logic, beyond the understanding as a conceptually derived version of visual reality. But his use of the term "grotesque," belabored throughout the first portion of the essay and supported by an elaborate definition drawn from extraneous sources, is clearly not at all what Fellini means by "grotesque" as he dictates to Maya. Fellini finds the grotesque intellectually disturbing. It is Fellini, not the viewer, who has come to "expect" certain norms from visual "reality."

8. This is where, for all his genius in other matters, Henri Bergson's sense of laughter is cold and dry, cynical. The "appeal" of the comic, he writes, "is to the intelligence, pure and simple." *Laughter* (1900) in *Comedy* (Garden City, N.Y.: Doubleday, 1956), p. 64. Bergson's words are pertinent here because they accurately describe Fellini's intellectual detachment from the visible creation. But when Federico Fellini's genius is taken into full account it is impossible not to concur with Free when he says, "If our culture is breaking down, it might be because we have forgotten how to laugh at ourselves. Such laughter is Fellini's strength." "Fellini's *I Clowns* and the Grotesque," in *Federico Fellini: Essays in Criticism*, p. 200.

9. I refer, for instance, to Paola in *La dolce vita* and to Claudia in *8½*, but not to, say, Susy in *Juliet of the Spirits*.

10. For a radically different and remarkably lucid account of the function of these archetypal "women-in-white," see Frank Burke, "The Three Phase Process and the White Clown-Auguste Relationship in Fellini's *The Clowns*," in *The 1977 Film Studies Annual: Part One, Explorations in National Cinemas* (Pleasantville, N.Y.: Redgrave Publishing Co., 1977), pp. 124-42.

11. See Stuart Rosenthal, *The Cinema of Federico Fellini* (Cranbury, N.J.: A. S. Barnes, 1976), pp. 95-96.

12. Much too much has been made of the white clown/Augusto relation in the small amount of serious criticism devoted to *The Clowns*. Fellini himself is the originator of such a reductive game. See *Fellini on Fellini*, trans. Isabel Quigley ([New York]: Delacorte Press, 1976), pp. 124-30. For other discussions, see Stuart Rosenthal, *The Cinema of Federico Fellini*, pp. 97-100; William J. Free, "Fellini's *I Clowns* and the Grotesque," in *Federico Fellini: Essays in Criticism*, pp. 192-95; and Burke, "Three Phase Process."

13. It is worth noting, as an example of Fellini's entrenched self-

concept, that he is obviously annoyed at the mispronunciation of his name ("Bellini") by the museum curator. He repeats his name to her: "Fellini, Fellini," insisting, that is, on his character, on his identity.

14. Frank Burke locates the clue to what is in this chapter termed *artificial narration* before Fellini's words reemerge to end the sequence. He points to the moment when the "lawyer" swings his gavel at the camera as signaling the "(self-) consciousness" of the sequence; see "The Three Phase Process and the White Clown-Auguste Relationship in Fellini's *The Clowns.*" While this is a trenchant observation, the fact remains that there is no intrinsic connection between Fellini the "director" and the camera. Therefore it is still possible to say that the more accurate way of seeing the artificial narration as a whole is by considering it as a sequence which begins and ends self-consciously. It begins with Fellini's elegy on "the clown" at the end of the historical mode, and it ends with Fellini's jealousy over the unmediated resurrection. But the action in between is what constitutes at once an advance in contrast to the historical narration, an outright assault on Fellini's claim to narrative supremecy, and a disclosure of the possibilities that can become actualities in and during the genial narration.

INDEX